THE OFFICIAL  GUIDE

GRAND PRIX 2008》》

This edition published in 2008 by
Carlton Books Limited
20 Mortimer Street
London W1T 3JW

10 9 8 7 6 5 4 3 2

itv SPORT

A CIP catalogue record for this book is available from
the British Library.

The publisher has taken reasonable steps to check
the accuracy of the facts contained herein at the
time of going to press, but cantake no responsibility
for any errors.

ISBN: 978-1-84442-051-3

Project Art Editor: Paul Chattaway
Designer: Ben Ruocco
Picture Research: Paul Langan
Production: Lisa Cook

Printed in Slovenia

Ferrari and McLaren were at each other's throats in 2007 and will be again this year.

THE OFFICIAL itv SPORT GUIDE

GRAND PRIX 2008»

BRUCE JONES

CARLTON
BOOKS

CONTENTS

LEFT: McLaren's Lewis Hamilton was the focus of attention last year and his every move will be followed as he tilts for the title in 2008.

OVERLEAF: The sights and sounds of watching a grand prix are unbeatable. This is the crowd soaking up the atmosphere at the Spanish GP.

ANALYSIS OF THE 2008 SEASON

Formula One offered its best racing for years in 2007 and looks set to be even more interesting as the top teams have been rejigged like seldom before by Fernando Alonso's departure from McLaren. Add to that rampant interest in Lewis Hamilton and a raft of technical changes and everything is wonderfully difficult to predict.

There has been a fulsome shuffling of the pack for 2008. Last-minute World Champion Kimi Raikkonen rightly stays put at Ferrari, as does Felipe Massa, but Fernando Alonso has quit McLaren to rejoin Renault, leaving last year's rookie hero Lewis Hamilton to be partnered by former Renault racer Heikki Kovalainen, showing how the effects of Alonso's departure have been felt far and wide.

Staying out of it, BMW Sauber who were fast and consistent in 2007, expect more of the same from Nick Heidfeld and Robert Kubica, while Renault will be desperate to bounce back with Alonso.

Williams share engines with Toyota, but look far more likely to land a sizeable haul of points, especially if Nico Rosberg continues to improve. Toyota has done nothing as yet to suggest that it will suddenly start challenging for race wins.

Red Bull Racing is sticking with David Coulthard and Mark Webber and hoping that its upswing of form in the final few races of 2007 can be continued. Its sister team, Scuderia Toro Rosso, has great hopes for Sebastian Vettel, while Sebastien Bourdais arrives with four straight Champ Car titles to his name.

Honda will be hoping for a transformation in form under the control of Ross Brawn who achieved so much at Benetton then Ferrari, with Jenson Button and Rubens Barrichello remaining on the driving force. It won't happen overnight, though. The other team using Honda V8s, Super Aguri Racing, remains strapped for cash, but it will be looking to break into the points again.

Although it looks as though there's a new team on the grid, in Force India F1, this is simply yet another rebadging of the team that was once Jordan and most recently Spyker. However, there was to have been an all-new team on the grid: Prodrive. Famed for its success in the FIA World Rally Championship and in sportscar racing, Prodrive had hoped to enter running McLaren chassis, but the long-running debate over the use of customer chassis – something that seemed to have been agreed at the Brazilian GP, then undone – may have delayed their arrival until 2009.

As the first season of a new Concorde Agreement, there are quite a raft of technical changes facing the teams, with the banning of traction control perhaps the most significant. Certainly, the older drivers are delighted by this, feeling that recent cars that have been allowed to run with this driver aid have made Formula One less of a step-up for rookies. Asking all drivers to demonstrate their throttle control will sort the men from the boys they say, and perhaps the results will be revealing.

All the teams will run a common ECU, as part of the cost-saving measures championed by FIA President Max Mosley. Chief among these budgetary changes is that gearboxes are now expected to last four races and engines still two, again with a 19,000rpm rev limit. Mosley has also pushed for the current engines to have their specifications frozen until 2017, but the teams want to be able to change after the end of next year.

Of the visible changes, the cars look marginally different as their cockpit sides have been raised by 25mm as a response to a near miss at last year's Australian GP when David Coulthard's Red Bull bounced on top of Alexander Wurz's Williams and came close to taking the Austrian's head off. Also, there's the procedural change, wherein the confusing and widely misunderstood fuel-burn element of the third qualifying session has been dropped and the session reduced from 15 minutes to 10 with the scrapping of the fuel credit system.

The tyre regulations remain the same, with Bridgestone supplying four control compounds (super-soft, soft, medium and hard), two of which being selected for any grand prix. Based on the findings from last year, there will be a tweak to the super-soft tyre to ensure it can work at all tracks.

While so much about 2007 was great, one thing that Formula One fans will hope not to endure this year is another spying scandal. It sullied the atmosphere, especially in the way with which it was handled.

FERRARI

Last year was a great year for Ferrari. With driver continuity while McLaren has lost one of its stars, the team from Maranello should have an advantage going into 2008, especially as Raikkonen is now fully integrated into the team after a shaky start.

Kimi Raikkonen ended last season on a high. Can he do so again?

Having been beaten by Renault in 2005 and 2006, and that was even with the mighty Michael Schumacher leading their attack, Ferrari were absolutely delighted to go back to the top last year. Their tally of nine wins from the 17 grands prix helped them to both the drivers' and constructors' titles after a mighty battle with McLaren. Rest assured, this battle is far from finished between Formula One's two heavyweights, so fireworks are all but guaranteed and every fraction of a second and scrap of racing circuit is going to be fought for.

With both Kimi Raikkonen and Felipe Massa staying for a second season together, there's no reason why one or other ought not end the year as world champion, and a tally of another nine wins is certainly not beyond them. Obviously, with Raikkonen having advanced through 2007 to bag the drivers' title after Massa upended the form book to set the pace in the first third of the campaign, the supposition must be that he is the bona fide number one within the team. So look for most of the effort from Maranello being focused on the Finn, even though the Brazilian is certainly a popular team member and also blessed with being managed by former team boss Jean Todt's son Nicolas.

Ferrari's success last year

PAST LEGENDS

This most archetypically Italian team has a history of fielding British drivers, and they have been successful for the men in red too. Not Michael Schumacher, seven world title successful, but title-bagging all the same. Mike Hawthorn was the first to strike, being crowned after a shoot-out in 1958. Peter Collins was a three-time race winner for Ferrari, but never a champion. While Tony Brooks, one of Hawthorn's rivals that afternoon, then joined up and won two races, but never the crown. John Surtees did though, striking gold in 1964 before quitting in 1966 after pointing out that the team was becoming wayward. Cliff Allison had already passed through and Mike Parkes was next to follow, but a host of British drivers including Derek Bell had a limited time there, often spending more time racing in sports cars. It wasn't until Nigel Mansell joined in 1989, though, that a British driver got a fair crack of the whip and winning first time out earned the love of the tifosi. Most recently, Eddie Irvine raced for Ferrari from 1996 to 1999, winning four races but having to settle for being runner-up in 1999.

carries added credit in that not only did they return to the top of the tree as Renault dropped away from their 2006 competitiveness and McLaren advanced, but they did so after rejigging their long-established senior line-up in which Ross Brawn masterminded all matters technical and how they were manifested on the track. Todt remained at the helm when Brawn departed for his year's sabbatical, with Amedeo Felisa being promoted to take some of his work load and Stefano Domenicali operating as sporting director. It was announced in November that Brawn would not be returning, and while Todt's role remained unconfirmed, Domenicali was promoted to fill Todt's role of Director of Ferrari's Gestione Sportive, Mario Almondo to operations director and Aldo Costa to technical director. Rest assured that these highly professional individuals will be doing their utmost to ensure that the ball isn't dropped again as it was last year when the pit crew forgot to refuel Massa in qualifying in Hungary.

In some ways, Massa will feel similar pressure in the year ahead as, following his departure from McLaren, Fernando Alonso is said to be eyeing a ride with Ferrari for 2009 and, even though Massa has a contract for that championship, Formula One is no respecter of such things and Ferrari wouldn't be expected to prevent such a 'dream team' of Raikkonen and Alonso from coming into force.

Another thing that Ferrari will be looking to avoid is what happened in their wind tunnel last April when a rolling road belt snapped and delayed their aero programme. Glance at the results and it was hard to detect at the time as Massa won in Bahrain and Spain, but the fact that Ferrari had to wait until July for its next win, in France after the arrival of a host of aero developments, gives evidence of the ground lost in Formula One's eternal quest to move forwards.

By adopting a longer than average wheelbase in 2007, Ferrari was very aero efficient and found an advantage on

tracks with longer fast corners, although it suffered over bumps and kerbs, but it has been decided to go for a shorter wheelbase on the F2008, something that has perhaps been forced on the design team by the banning of traction control.

Whatever happens at Ferrari in 2008, they won't want another

setback such as the one they suffered when their floors were adjudged too flexible after the opening grand prix in Australia and they definitely won't want another scandal emanating from sensitive material being passed to a rival team by one of their own employees.

FOR THE RECORD

Country of origin:	Italy
Team base:	Maranello, Italy
Telephone:	(39) 0536 949111
Website:	WWW.FERRARIWORLD.COM
Active in Formula One:	From 1950
Grands Prix contested:	758
Wins:	201
Pole positions:	195
Fastest laps:	203

2007 DRIVERS & RESULTS

Driver	Nationality	Races	Wins	Pts	Pos
Felipe Massa	Brazilian	17	3	94	4th
Kimi Raikkonen	Finnish	17	6	110	1st

THE TEAM

Chairman & CEO:	Luca di Montezemolo
Team principal:	Stefano Domenicali
Director of operations:	Mario Almondo
Technical director:	Aldo Costa
Engine director:	Gilles Simon
Head of track operations:	Luca Baldisserri
Car design consultant:	Rory Byrne
Chief designer:	Nicolas Tombazis
Chief aerodynamicist:	John Iley
Race & technical manager:	David Lloyd
Test drivers:	Luca Badoer
Chassis:	Ferrari F2008
Engine:	Ferrari V8
Tyres:	Bridgestone

Mike Hawthorn was the first British driver to win the title with Ferrari.

KIMI RAIKKONEN

Here is a driver who had future world champion writ large upon him from his early days. Twice that title escaped when he raced for McLaren and last year seemed to be another lost cause, but he was a worthy champion at the kill.

Some drivers have become world champion without being the best, but blessed with being with the right team at the right time. Fortunately for the purists, last year's title-winning success with Ferrari has meant that Kimi will now never be consigned to the opposite class: the ones who were easily good enough, but never had the equipment beneath them to do the job.

Kimi will never be an articulate champion for, although a smile lit up his face when he beat all the odds to wrest the title from McLaren's drivers at Interlagos last October, and he even offered more than a few sentences of explanation to the media, taciturn is Kimi's default option.

Life at Ferrari is suiting him better than it did at McLaren, but it wasn't always like that during his first year with the men in red. At the Canadian GP in June, there was even talk of him being replaced, as Felipe Massa was outperforming him. Add to that the fact that Massa was managed by Jean Todt's son, and imagine how Kimi felt.

Kimi knows what it's like to be the world champion and he rather likes it...

Whatever happened next, whether the arrival of new mods for the car or simply a new attitude, it certainly worked, for Kimi won the next two races on the trot.

It's clear that Kimi now loves Ferrari and Ferrari loves Kimi. And, should they provide him with another good car, he'll be in with a shot at the title again.

TRACK NOTES

Nationality:	FINNISH
Born:	17 OCTOBER 1979, ESPOO, FINLAND
Website:	WWW.KIMIRAIKKONEN.COM
Teams:	SAUBER 2001, McLaren 2002-2006, FERRARI 2007-2008

CAREER RECORD

First Grand Prix:	2001 AUSTRALIAN GP
Grand Prix starts:	122
Grand Prix wins:	15
	2003 Malaysian GP, 2004 Belgian GP, 2005 Spanish GP, Monaco GP, Canadian GP, Hungarian GP, Turkish GP, Belgian GP, Japanese GP, 2007 Australian GP, French GP, British GP, Belgian GP, Chinese GP, Brazilian GP
Poles:	14
Fastest laps:	25
Points:	446
Honours:	2007 FORMULA ONE WORLD CHAMPION, 2005 & 2003 FORMULA ONE RUNNER-UP, 2000 BRITISH FORMULA RENAULT CHAMPION, 1999 BRITISH FORMULA RENAULT WINTER SERIES CHAMPION, 1998 EUROPEAN SUPER A KART RUNNER-UP & FINNISH KART CHAMPION & NORDIC KART CHAMPION

CAREER HISTORY

Kimi was Mr Karting in Finland, winning the national Formula A title in 1998 and finishing second in the European series. Fortunately for Kimi, former racer Steve Robertson decided to help him into car racing. This came in 1999, but he quit after four British Formula Renault races, considering the team less than competitive. Kimi returned to contest the British winter series and won all four rounds. Revamped by this, he returned for a second crack at the full British series in 2000 with Manor Motorsport and became a dominant champion. Formula Three would have been the obvious progression, but Robertson talked Sauber into giving him a test run. Kimi didn't disappoint, as he landed a ride for 2001, after only 23 car races... McLaren snapped him up for 2003, and Kimi was runner-up to Michael Schumacher. He was second overall again in 2005 before joining Ferrari for 2007.

FELIPE MASSA

Although he was out of the reckoning as the season approached its finale, Felipe came of age in 2007 and proved himself capable of fighting with the best. He will have to fight hard in 2008 as his seat at Ferrari is apparently sought by Alonso.

Imagine how it felt. You'd won the final race of 2006 and Mr Win-It-All Michael Schumacher had retired, leaving you in a far stronger position with your team, Ferrari. The highly-ranked Kimi Raikkonen was arriving from McLaren and was expected to fill the roll vacated by Schuey.

Obviously, you wanted to prevent this, stop yourself being subsumed to the role of number two again. One race in to your 2007 campaign, Kimi had kicked off with a win, you with a troubled sixth after having to start from the back of the grid. Maybe you tried too hard next time out, in Malaysia, turning pole position to an eventual fifth place. Yet, when the dust settled in Bahrain after round three, you were a winner again, Kimi off the pace in third.

This was the story of Felipe's coming of age. Certainly, he was embedded at Ferrari, loved by the team and fully conversant of its workings while Kimi still had to settle in. Now was the time to strike and victory next time out in Spain was embellished by Kimi leaving the circuit straight after

Felipe started strongly in 2007 and won't want to have to play second fiddle again

he retired, something that Michael would never have done. With Lewis Hamilton also putting one over his more fancied team leader Fernando Alonso at McLaren, roles were being reversed.

The dream didn't last for Felipe and a non-score in Hungary and retirement at Monza took him out of the title chase. Showing how transient things can be in Formula One, Felipe and manager were even spotted talking to rival teams before his contract was extended to 2010. It might have been worthwhile as many expect Alonso to have taken his place alongside Raikkonen for next year.

TRACK NOTES

Nationality:	BRAZILIAN
Born:	25 APRIL 1981, SAO PAULO, BRAZIL
Website:	WWW.FELIPEMASSA.COM
Teams:	SAUBER 2002 & 2004-2005, FERRARI 2006-08

CAREER RECORD	
First Grand Prix:	2001 AUSTRALIAN GP
Grand Prix starts:	88
Grand Prix wins:	5
	2006 Turkish GP, Brazilian GP, 2007 Bahrain GP, Spanish GP, Turkish GP
Poles:	9
Fastest laps:	8
Points:	201
Honours:	2001 EUROPEAN FORMULA 3000 CHAMPION, 2000 EUROPEAN & ITALIAN FORMULA RENAULT CHAMPION, 1999 BRAZILIAN FORMULA CHEVROLET CHAMPION

CAREER HISTORY

Kimi Raikkonen set a trend when he was plucked from obscurity by Sauber to race in Formula One in 2001. A year later, Felipe had followed his lead to break into the sport's top category with the Swiss team. He was little known as he'd had not featured in the acknowledged feeder categories. After coming through karting, he'd done well to become European Formula Renault champion. But Felipe skipped Formula Three. Instead, due to budgetary constraints, he raced in the second division European Formula 3000 series – not to be mistaken with the FIA International Formula 3000 series. This he won, earning a Sauber test, and he was in. Although dropped for being erratic, Felipe was back with Sauber after spending 2003 testing for Ferrari. When Rubens Barrichello moved on, Felipe joined Ferrari full-time, taking his first win in Turkey in 2006.

BMW SAUBER

BMW Sauber made massive strides in 2007, establishing themselves as the best of the rest behind the Ferraris and McLarens. The measure of the team will come this year as Nick Heidfeld and Robert Kubica start pushing for race victories.

Nick Heidfeld was a star in 2007. Now he must move to the front.

Such has been the progress of the team put together by BMW motorsport boss Mario Theissen that it's already, just over two years in, hard to remember the connection with the team from which it metamorphosed: Sauber.

Yes, the white and dark blue livery is vastly fresher than the mid blue mess of the Sauber colours of old, but the differences lie far deeper than that. The money that finally gave the team a new burst of life and bought it facilities of which it could only ever have dreamed has been a boost, to say nothing of the considerable swelling of the work force. However, it's the work ethos and direction that

Theissen has brought to the team that has created the most impetus.

Willy Rampf, technical director both before and after the take-over by BMW, relishes the transformation and the fact that he has more people to delegate the work to so that he can concentrate on the key job in hand: the creation of a car capable of going for gold.

Chief designer Jorg Zander left early last year to join Honda and long-time Sauber employee Christoph Zimmerman has been elevated from within to fill the post, with Mariano Alperin-Bruvera travelling the opposite direction to Zander to join from Honda to head up the

PAST LEGENDS

Think of Sauber from its launch into Formula One in 1993 to the moment that the cars turned from dark to light with the arrival of BMW in 2006, and only a few names stand out. BMW Sauber team leader Nick Heidfeld is one and fellow German Heinz-Harald Frentzen another as they guided Sauber from the midfield to the podium, with Frentzen the first to achieve this for the Swiss team with third in the 1995 Italian GP. Johnny Herbert, who grabbed the next one, for third at Monaco in 1996, and the following one, too, at Hungary in 1997. Jean Alesi who took a pair of second-place finishes for the team at Austria in 1998 and then in France the year after that. But, for sheer perseverance, it's Heidfeld who will always stand out, especially for his startling form through 2007 when he was the best of the rest behind the Ferrari and McLaren drivers. After spending his maiden season with the team, in 2001, Kimi Raikkonen went on to become World Champion with Ferrari, something that fellow former Sauber racer Felipe Massa is also hoping to do.

aerodynamcis division.

Expect much of the gain that is sought from the F1.08 to come from the aerodynamics, as one of the major areas of growth has come from the team's wind tunnel staff being expanded from 35 to 85, meaning that the tunnel can now be run six days per week, with three shifts utilising it 24 hours a day, emphasising how far design has come from the days in the 1960s when Lotus supremo Colin Chapman would sketch his latest brainwave onto a fag packet and hand it to someone in the workshop to knock together.

That BMW Sauber's latest supercomputer is three times faster than its predecessor and is further proof that Formula One teams continue to push for ever more accurate simulation results to prevent them taking an expensive and time-consuming design cul-de-sac.

When a team is advancing, as BMW Sauber did from fifth overall to second last year after the confiscation of McLaren's points, having continuity on the driver front can be a helping hand. With this is mind, and anxious to keep Nick Heidfeld's chassis development capabilities, he and Robert Kubica will partner each other for a second full season, with the Pole relieved that he is unlikely to have to spend much of the season adapting his driving style to suit the tyres as he did last year when everyone raced on spec tyres from Bridgestone that didn't suit his favoured style of aggressive early turn-in.

One advantage that they appeared to have in 2007 will be denied the team this year by a rule change, and this is the excellent getaways that their electronics enabled them to have.

After the drivers decided early last season that they wanted as much track time as possible, the services of a third driver at grands prix was scrapped, with Sebastian Vettel being pushed to the sidelines, so don't expect that role to be offered again as the drivers want to do the set-up work and tyre selection.

While BMW Sauber would most likely be pleased with a repeat performance, having exceeded their own expectations in 2007, they are also aware that Renault underperformed and will be more of a handful this time around. To stay ahead, BMW Sauber will need to demonstrate even greater speed and more of their impressive reliability, and to prove how keen they were, they were one of the teams that turned their attention away from developing their 2007 car in the closing races of last year to focus on this year's challenge.

Johnny Herbert raced to third place for Sauber at Monaco in 1996.

FOR THE RECORD

Country of origin:	Switzerland
Team base:	Hinwil, Switzerland
Telephone:	(41) 44 937 9000
Website:	www.bmw-sauber-f1.com
Active in Formula One:	From 1993 (as Sauber until 2005)
Grands Prix contested:	252
Wins:	0
Pole positions:	0
Fastest laps:	0

2007 DRIVERS & RESULTS

Driver	Nationality	Races	Wins	Pts	Pos
Nick Heidfeld	German	17	0	61	5th
Robert Kubica	Polish	16	0	39	6th
Sebastian Vettel	German	1	-	1	14th

THE TEAM

Team principal:	Mario Theissen
Technical director:	Willy Rampf
Chief designer:	Christoph Zimmerman
Head of powertrain:	Markus Duesman
Head of aerodynamics:	Willem Toet
Head of track engineering:	Mike Krack
Project manager:	Walter Riedl
Team manager:	Beat Zehnder
Test driver:	Sebastian Vettel
Chassis:	F1.08
Engine:	BMW V8
Tyres:	Bridgestone

NICK HEIDFELD

Nick had to deliver in 2007 to save his reputation, and deliver he did, rising to the challenge of picking up reaching the podium if the Ferraris or McLarens failed. With his reputation restored, he's even talking of a title challenge in 2009.

It might have been the arrival of Kubica midway through 2006 after the departure of the dispirited Jacques Villeneuve that did it, but Nick looked hungrier at the start of 2007 than he had since his arrival in Formula One back in 2000.

Combine this with the fact that BMW's financial and engineering muscle was starting to take the BMW Sauber team to a level on which it had never operated before and you can understand why his optimism was bubbling over after his first three grands prix produced three fourth place finishes. The most satisfying of these was in Bahrain when he passed Fernando Alonso's McLaren around the outside mid-race. It was audacious, excellently executed and a definite feather in his cap. In short, it cemented Nick's place with the team.

Not that there wasn't talk of a possible switch to Toyota for 2008 in place of Ralf Schumacher, but Nick is more than happy to be continuing with a team very much on the up. It's also a team of which Nick is a major part, having spent 2001 to 2003 with

Nick was rapid and consistent last year, but will he be in a position to press for wins in 2008?

the team from Hinwil when they were just plain old Sauber.

To keep Nick on his toes, his deal is for 2008 only, but he is going to be on his toes anyway as he knows that his record

of 134 grand prix starts without a win is propelling him towards the top of a chart that no one wants to top. For the record, Nick ranks fifth and a winless season will leave him behind only Andrea de Cesaris (208 grand prix starts without a win) and Martin Brundle (158).

TRACK NOTES

Nationality:	GERMAN
Born:	10 MAY 1977, MOENCHENGLADBACH, GERMANY
Website:	WWW.NICKHEIDFELD.DE
Teams:	PROST 2000, SAUBER 2001-2003, JORDAN 2004, WILLIAMS 2005, BMW SAUBER 2006-2008

CAREER RECORD

First Grand Prix:	2000 AUSTRALIAN GP
Grand Prix starts:	134
Grand Prix wins:	0
	best result: second, 2007 Canadian GP, 2005 Monaco & European GPs
Poles:	1
Fastest laps:	0
Points:	140
Honours:	1999 FORMULA 3000 CHAMPION, 1998 FORMULA 3000 RUNNER-UP, 1997 GERMAN FORMULA THREE CHAMPION, 1995 GERMAN FORMULA FORD RUNNER-UP, 1994 GERMAN FF1600 CHAMPION

CAREER HISTORY

The early stages of Nick's career, in karting and junior single-seaters, went like clockwork, with Formula Ford titles in 1994 and 1995. He was instantly on the pace in Formula Three and was German champion at his second attempt, also winning the Monaco support race. Juan Pablo Montoya beat Nick to the Formula 3000 title in 1998, but he took the 1999 crown. Having had two years as a test driver for McLaren, Nick made his Formula One racing debut with Prost in 2000. Joining Sauber for 2001 was a good move and he ranked eighth overall. But the team dropped away and so did he. A year with Jordan in 2004 showed he still had the ability, even in a weak car. With Williams using BMW engines in 2005, the team needed a German driver. He placed second at Monaco and the Nurburgring, where he started from pole. Nick moved with BMW to Sauber for 2006.

ROBERT KUBICA

Those expecting race wins from this the most startling rookie of 2006 weren't being realistic, but Robert put some valuable experience under his belt last year, most especially in the area of handling a car that he found tricky to drive.

At the start of 2007, Robert was struggling. That podium position in only his third Formula One outing at Monza in 2006 had made him think that anything was possible, the pace of the Ferraris and McLaren withstanding, but the change to a different type of Bridgestone tyre appeared to catch him out. It was said by technical director Willy Rampf that they didn't suit the Pole's driving style of turning in aggressively and it took a while to sort the car's set-up to suit him.

Then, just as Robert was settling back into form expected of him, came the Canadian GP. He certainly won't want a repeat of the horrendous and definitely life-threatening accident that he suffered after he clipped Jarno Trulli's Toyota. At the moment of his 145mph impact with the wall on the approach to the 3 hairpin, he experienced 75g. That he walked away from hospital with little more than a shaking is testament to the strength of the cars which is something that he probably won't be in a

Robert bounced back from his accident in 2007 and knows that he must continue his progress.

rush to check to such a degree in future.

To bounce back two races later, in France, with fourth place on his return said a lot about the mettle of the man.

Like team-mate Nick Heidfeld, Robert's contract is only for this year, so his target has to be to appear on the podium as often as possible and be ready to claim BMW Sauber's maiden victory if the opportunity should present itself. Should this happen, Poland will erupt with pride. For now, though, his principal target is to outscore his team-mate and work forward from there.

TRACK NOTES

Nationality:	POLISH
Born:	7 DECEMBER 1984, CRACOW, POLAND
Website:	WWW.KUBICA.PL
Teams:	BMW SAUBER 2006-2008

CAREER RECORD

First Grand Prix:	2006 HUNGARIAN GP
Grand Prix starts:	22
Wins:	0
	best result: third, 2006 Italian GP
Pole positions:	0
Fastest laps:	0
Points:	45
Honours:	2005 WORLD SERIES BY RENAULT CHAMPION, 1999 GERMAN & ITALIAN KARTING CHAMPION, 1999 MONACO KART CUP WINNER, 1998 ITALIAN KARTING CHAMPION, 1998 MONACO KART CUP WINNER, 1997 POLISH KARTING CHAMPION

CAREER HISTORY

Injuries in any sport can interrupt or end a career, so Robert was most lucky that a broken arm suffered, ironically, as a passenger in a road accident didn't cost him too much momentum. This came in 2003, after he had already starred in karting, principally in Italy in 1998 after he'd dominated the Polish scene, also winning the Monaco Kart Trophy. He had a near repeat in 1999 and was fourth in the Formula A world championship in 2000. After racing in Formula Renault in Italy in 2001 and finishing as runner-up in 2002, Robert landed Renault backing, which he took with him into European Formula Three in 2003. That broken arm made him miss the first seven rounds, but he'd won a race by season's end. His second year of Formula Three was less successful, but Robert got back won the 2005 World Series by Renault. Then came his Formula One break with BMW Sauber in mid-2006, as replacement for Jacques Villeneuve.

RENAULT

World champions in 2005 and 2006, Renault fell from grace with an inherent design flaw, making it hard to get used to the Bridgestone tyres. With Alonso and Nelson Piquet Jr on its books, the team is confident that it will get back to winning form.

Renault fell away in 2007 and knows that it must raise its game.

Double world champion Fernando Alonso had departed, for McLaren, but Renault were still reckoning on having a strong season in 2007. How wrong they were, as the R27 was tricky to drive as it was unstable and seemingly handled different from corner to corner. This was all because of an aerodynamic shortfall inherent to the design and took half the season to get on top of, leaving the team frustrated that it couldn't get the most out of the Bridgestone tyres, which was a huge frustration after their relationship with Michelin had been so strong. For a team that likes to go forward, having to spend much of the year backtracking to find the root of the problem was maddening and certainly hampered their typical seasonal development.

The brains of Renault, and there are a good few wise heads who work well together in a team that works as a team rather than as a melding of egos, will have worked flat-out since last summer to make sure the R28 puts them back on track. Indeed, they chose from August to concentrate on getting the R28 right rather than develop the R27, so perhaps incoming president Bernard Rey, who took over from Alain Dassas, will have reason to smile.

Executive director of engineering Pat Symonds started changing the workforce

PAST LEGENDS

Until Fernando Alonso guided the French marque to a world title double in 2005 and 2006, Renault's greatest successes had come as engine supplier to Williams and Benetton, which yielded world a stream of titles starting in 1992 (for Nigel Mansell), then in 1993 (Alain Prost), 1995 (Michael Schumacher), 1996 (Damon Hill) and 1997 (Jacques Villeneuve). However, the driver who really propelled Renault to the front in Formula One was Prost when he was racing for Renault itself before it ceased running a team at the end of the 1985 campaign. It was the team's first racer, Jean-Pierre Jabouille who scored its first win, in 1979, two years after its launch, before team-mate Rene Arnoux became the main man through 1980. But it was Prost who really gave Renault momentum when he joined in 1981. The world title ought to have been his and Renault's in 1983, but they lost out to Nelson Piquet and Brabham at the South African finale. Of course, Renault did come back, in 2002, but this was merely a rebadging of the Benetton team rather than a revival of the French team of old.

last year. Or, more to the point, how they fitted together, as he moved aside a bit and chief race engineer Alan Permane took up some of the workload, allowing Pat to look ahead to other areas such as analysing future rules and regulations. Deputy technical director James Allison will be hoping for a quieter year, after spending much of 2007 working backwards to find the source of the fault, which came at the aerodynamic modelling stage. Director of aerodynamic technology Dino Toso was also involved in the great aero investigation and is now working on the team's new Euro 50 million CFD facility to ensure that such events don't happen again.

As if this aero problem hadn't been such a thorn in their side, the loss of Alonso was keenly felt. Giancarlo Fisichella worked hard and had the experience not to overdrive the car and, in fact, drive within its initial limits, while new boy Heikki Kovalainen was all over the place. Team principal Flavio Briatore was eventually able to see the funny side once the team got the car balanced by the Candian GP, joking that it had been Heikki's brother behind the wheel up until then. Indeed, the fourth and fifth place finishes the Finn collected in Montreal then Indianapolis matched Giancarlo's early-season results from Monaco and Melbourne, but from this point he became the team's leading driver, gathering the team's best result of second place in Japan.

By year's end, Renault were fourth fastest on the track behind the Ferraris, McLarens and BMW Saubers, so the year wasn't a total disaster, but team harmony was unsettled by suggestions that Alonso, so unhappy at McLaren, might be rejoining for 2008. If so, would Fisichella or Kovalainen be pushed to one side? It later proved that both would and test driver Nelson Piquet Jr would be stepping up to partner Alonso.

Then came confirmation that Renault was being investigated for the alleged transfer of technical information from McLaren, but it was cleared.

FOR THE RECORD

Country of origin:	England
Team base:	Enstone, England
Telephone:	(44) 01608 678000
Website:	www.ing-renaultf1.com
Active in Formula One:	From 1977-85 and from 2002
Grands Prix contested:	238*
Wins:	33
Pole positions:	49
Fastest laps:	27

* NOTE THAT THESE FIGURES DO NOT INCLUDE THE 238 RACES THE TEAM RAN AS BENETTON

2007 DRIVERS & RESULTS

Driver	Nationality	Races	Wins	Pts	Pos
Giancarlo Fisichella	Italian	17	-	21	8th
Heikki Kovalainen	Finnish	17	-	30	7th

THE TEAM

President:	Bernard Rey
Managing director:	Flavio Briatore
Deputy managing director (engine):	Rob White
Deputy managing director (support operations):	Andre Laine
Technical director:	Bob Bell
Executive director of engineering:	Pat Symonds
Deputy technical director:	James Allison
Head of trackside operations:	Denis Chevrier
Chief designer:	Tim Densham
Chief engineer:	Alan Permane
Team manager:	Steve Nielsen
Test drivers:	Romain Grosjean
Chassis:	Renault R28
Engine:	Renault V8
Tyres:	Bridgestone

Alain Pros failed to become world champion for Renault in 1983.

FERNANDO ALONSO

It could have been a marriage made in heaven and his first year with McLaren crowned by his third straight world title. But that is not how it panned out and Fernando is going to have a clean year back with Renault to restore his name.

The difference that 17 grands prix can make is astonishing. It can turn a rookie into a superstar, like Lewis Hamilton. Conversely, it can turn a grand prix winner into someone whose services are no longer required, like Ralf Schumacher. Or it can turn the driver everyone rated, even as a good sort, into a petulant, almost cartoon-style baddie, like Fernando.

Quite how the year in which he was joining the team he'd always wanted to race for McLaren and could have turned him into a three-time world champion failed to deliver, albeit by only two points, will remain as one of the more interesting parables of grand prix history.

As soon as he lost his cool after the first four races as Hamilton began to challenge him, his manner turned from delight at being with a winning team to one of petulance. And, with the change of demeanour, Fernando's stock plummeted. His attempts to scare McLaren boss Ron Dennis into supporting him alone in an ill-advised meeting on the morning of

Fernando is back and will be hoping for a less tumultuous time than he had last year.

the Hungarian GP horrified everyone. And so it was, by last December, his return to Renault – perhaps only for 2008 before moving to Ferrari next year – was inked in. However, for all the acrimony, there is no

doubting that Fernando remains one of the fastest drivers, a fearsome competitor with a killer instinct allied to his natural speed, and this is why Renault fought so hard to land his services for 2008.

TRACK NOTES

Nationality:	SPANISH
Born: 2	9 JULY, 1981, OVIEDO, SPAIN
Website:	WWW.FERNANDOALONSO.COM
Teams:	MINARDI 2001, RENAULT 2003-2006,
	McLAREN 2007, RENAULT 2008

CAREER RECORD	
First Grand Prix:	2001 AUSTRALIAN GP
Grand Prix starts:	105
Wins:	19
	2003 Hungarian GP, 2005 Malaysian GP, Bahrain GP, San Marino GP, European GP, French GP, German GP, Chinese GP, 2006 Bahrain GP, Australian GP, Spanish GP, Monaco GP, British GP, Canadian GP, Japanese GP, 2007 Malaysian GP, Monaco GP, European GP, Italian GP)
Pole positions:	16
Fastest laps:	11
Points:	580
Honours:	2005 & 2006 FORMULA ONE WORLD CHAMPION, 1999 FORMULA NISSAN CHAMPION, 1997 ITALIAN & SPANISH KART CHAMPION, 1996 WORLD & SPANISH KART CHAMPION, 1995 & 1994

CAREER HISTORY

Anyone with two Formula One titles by the time they're 25 must be special, and one glance at Fernando's karting record shows that his ability was there from the start. He was Spanish junior champion then world champion in 1996. He had to wait until 1999 to be old enough to race cars, but to say he was more than ready is an understatement as he stepped straight into the Formula Nissan championship and won the title ahead of far more experienced racers. Formula 3000 – then Formula One's feeder formula – was next and he got better and better, thrashing his rivals at Spa-Francorchamps. Paul Stoddart picked him for Minardi for 2001 and Renault soon signed him. This meant spending 2002 as test driver, but he was racing for the team in 2003 and scored his first win, in Hungary. World titles followed in 2005 and 2006 before his move to McLaren.

NELSON PIQUET JR

The contract was in his attache case, but Nelsinho had to wait and wait while Fernando Alonso decided what he would be doing in 2008. Eventually, in December, Renault announced that he would be stepping up from their test team.

Yup, here's another son of a racing driver father, in this instance three-time Formula One World Champion Nelson Piquet (crowned in 1981, 1983 and 1987), but Nelsinho has plenty to offer.

The 22-year-old with the film star looks has been quietly gaining Formula One experience for the past year, with Renault, and had done enough to sign a contract that guarantees him a race ride in 2008.

When Giancarlo Fisichella's form fell away through last year, there was even talk that he would be promoted early. But then the scenario altered when it became clear that Fernando Alonso would be quitting McLaren and wanted to return to the team that he had left at the end of 2006. While it was likely that Fisichella was on the way out, that still left the matter of the driver who had morphed into Renault's number one driver: Heikki Kovalainen. While the team was scrabbling around to find the money for Alonso's retainer, Reanult must

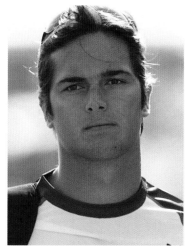

Nelsinho knows the team from being its test driver and must now deliver in the races.

have considered whether it would sell more road cars in Brazil or Finland and come up with the obvious answer. Add to that the fact that Nelsinho would more likely play the role of faithful number two, and you will understand why the decision was made.

Nelsinho will now be able to renew his rivalry with erstwhile GP2 rival Lewis Hamilton, to whom he finished as runner-up in 2006, scoring four wins.

Those who have never seen him race will be in for a treat, as he is like Hamilton, a master of the overtaking art, something that he showed to good effect when A1GP kicked off in 2005, guiding the Brazilian car to two wins at the Brands Hatch opener.

TRACK NOTES

Nationality:	BRAZILIAN
Born:	25 JULY, 1984, HEIDELBERG, GERMANY
Website:	WWW.PIQUETSPORTS.COM.BR
Teams:	2008 RENAULT

CAREER RECORD

FIRST GRAND PRIX:	2008 AUSTRALIAN GP
Grand Prix starts:	0
Grand Prix wins:	0
Poles:	0
Fastest laps:	0
Points:	0
Honours:	2006 GP2 RUNNER-UP, 2004 BRITISH FORMULA THREE CHAMPION, 2002 SOUTH AMERICAN FORMULA THREE CHAMPION

CAREER HISTORY

Like so many other 'sons-of', it was always likely that Nelsinho (little Nelson) would try kart racing. This he did in Brazil from the age of 10, and cars inevitably followed as soon as he was old enough in the second half of 2001. The trademark of Nelsinho's early career was never to be underprepared, and he tested at every opportunity, helping him to land the South American Formula Three title in 2002. Then he followed the path that his father Nelson had taken with such success in the late 1970s and headed for Britain. His first year of British Formula Three was spent learning the tracks, ranking third overall. In 2004, though, the British title was his. He then tested with BAR in 2005, raced in GP2 for the family Piquet Sports team, winning at Spa-Francorchamps to rank eighth, and starred in A1GP for Team Brazil. This set up 2006 as his make-or-break season as he accelerated towards Formula One, but there was nothing that he could do to keep Hamilton from the title.

WILLIAMS

Williams showed fortitude and direction last autumn when it hung on to the services of the talismanic Nico Rosberg and also a nod to youth in signing Kazuki Nakajima. The team's target for 2008 is to rank in the top-three overall.

Nico Rosberg is confident that the team is heading back to the front.

It's safe to say that the driver market came to a standstill in the weeks following last year's final round when it became clear that Fernando Alonso was going to be parting company with McLaren. It took an age to find out where he was heading and every delay prevented other teams from completing their plans. After all, many wanted the Spaniard and some of those same teams wanted to keep their most treasured drivers from breaking their contracts and leaping at the now-vacated McLaren seat. The driver most heavily tipped to be joining Lewis Hamilton was Nico Rosberg, but Sir Frank Williams and Patrick Head weren't keen to lose the driver many see as their crown jewel: Nico.

So, while other dithered, Williams earned the plaudits for firming up its line-up for 2008, with Rosberg back for a third season and Kazuki Nakajima stepping up from the test team after his strong showing on his grand prix debut at last year's final round. That Toyota back Nakajima is certainly a help financially to this Toyota-powered team, a team that is climbing back to where it is accustomed of performing, that's to say at the sharp end of the field.

There were personnel changes early last year, with Ed Wood taking over from Gavin Fisher as chief designer and Jon

PAST LEGENDS

It's fitting that the two drivers who have scored the most points for this most British of teams are both British. They are Nigel Mansell and Damon Hill, who landed a Formula One title apiece in 1992 and 1996 respectively, and could both have become multiple world champions for the men from Grove if fate hadn't struck as it did. David Coulthard was also a winner for Williams in the mid-1990s and might have become world champion too if he hadn't elected to move for 1996 to a McLaren team in the doldrums. Williams' British connection continued when Jenson Button made the big leap from Formula Three in 2001, but the team couldn't guide him to victory. Perhaps the biggest shame of all was that the first driver that Frank ran – Piers Courage – was killed in the 1970 Dutch GP when Frank ran in Formula One on a shoestring budget and yet helped Piers to score a pair of second place finishes in 1969 when running him in a privately-entered Brabham. It wasn't until 1977 that Frank joined forces with Patrick Head to form the team as we know it today.

Tomlinson joining Loic Bigois in the aerodynamics department. The first fruits of their labour should be apparent in this year's chassis, the FW30.

Also, Sam Michael – who stretched himself too thin in 2006 – gained useful assistance at the races from Rod Nelson. Senior systems engineer John Russell deserves considerable praise as the team came away with a vastly superior finishing record of just four technical failures compared to 11 in 2006. Adopting a less complicated seamless shift was among the improvements, along with the way the Toyota engine was packaged. Add to this advance, the fact that Alexander Wurz used his canny racing skills to pick his way up the order to third in the much interrupted Canadian GP and then Rosberg fought his way past the BMW Saubers in Brazil to finish fourth and the progress was there for all to see, with eighth place overall in the 2006 constructors' championship being turned into fourth overall last year (boosted one position by McLaren's removal from the points table), scoring three times as many points.

Looking ahead, technical director Sam Michael said that the FW30 will follow the trend of running more downforce than before to help the drivers to make up for the loss of traction control.

Williams continues to benefit from an ever more productive relationship with Toyota and the use of Toyota's dynos at Cologne has been a big help. There will always remain the tricky situation of Toyota-powered Williams beating the works Toyota team, but hopefully the Japanese manufacturer will simply be happy for success from whichever team achieves it.

For now, though, everyone at Williams will be hoping that they can close down the 1s per lap average speed differential between them and arch-rivals Ferrari and McLaren so that they can start visiting the podium on merit.

FOR THE RECORD

Country of origin:	England
Team base:	Grove, England
Telephone:	(44) 01235 777700
Website:	WWW.WILLIAMSF1.COM
Active in Formula One:	From 1972
Grands Prix contested:	550
Wins:	113
Pole positions:	125
Fastest laps:	129

2007 DRIVERS & RESULTS

Driver	Nationality	Races	Wins	Pts	Pos
Kazuki Nakajima	Japanese	1	-	-	n/a
Nico Rosberg	German	17	-	20	9th
Alexander Wurz	Austrian	16	-	13	11th

THE TEAM

Team principal:	Sir Frank Williams
Director of engineering:	Patrick Head
Chief executive officer:	Adam Parr
Technical director:	Sam Michael
Chief operating officer:	Alex Burns
Chief designer:	Ed Wood
Head of aerodynamics:	Jon Tomlinson
Senior systems engineer:	John Russell
Chief operations engineer:	Rod Nelson
Team manager:	Tim Newton
Test driver:	Nico Hulkenberg
Chassis:	Williams FW30
Engine:	Toyota V8
Tyres:	Bridgestone

Nigel Mansell remains one of the most successful Williams drivers.

NICO ROSBERG

Two years in Formula One and no race victories is Nico's record so far, but there are many in the paddock who reckon that he will become a grand prix winner as soon as Williams manage to advance to supply him with the tools with which to do the job.

Despite scoring only four points and ranking 17th overall in his debut season of Formula One in 2006, there were many people singing Nico's praises. Last year, he scored five times that tally and advanced to ninth overall, but still the praises come flooding in for the German.

Indeed, he was considered hot property in the immediate wake of last season when teams were trying to snap him up for 2008 in the driver market confusion following Fernando Alonso's split with McLaren.

Much credibility was given to Nico leaving Williams to take Alonso's seat at McLaren for 2008, but that was without considering not only that Williams want to hang on to their star in the making, but that Nico's shrewd father Keke – World Champion in 1982 – wasn't keen on his 22-year-old partnering Lewis Hamilton again, as the Briton had had the upper hand whenever that had happened in karting and Formula Three.

Nico is maturing and remains Williams' greatest assets, but he needs podiums.

The key to why Nico is in such demand is that he can qualify well, learning to handle last year's spec Bridgestone tyres with aplomb, and his race craft is ever improving, with his battle to catch then pass the BMW Saubers in last year's Brazilian finale a clear example. That fourth place finish was the best result of his campaign, but just as impressive was his run of four straight sixth and seventh place finishes between the Hungaroring and Spa-Francorchamps, showing how he was driving cleanly as securing the best finishes possible for his Williams at that time. And that's all that any team boss can ask.

So, if Williams clicks in 2008, look out for Nico's golden locks on the podium.

TRACK NOTES

Nationality:	GERMAN
Born:	27 JUNE 1985, WIESBADEN, GERMANY
Website:	WWW.NICOROSBERG.COM
Teams:	WILLIAMS 2006-2008

CAREER RECORD

First Grand Prix:	2006 BAHRAIN GP
Grand Prix starts:	35
Grand Prix wins:	0
	best result: fourth, 2007 Brazilian GP
Poles:	0
Fastest laps:	1
Points:	24
Honours:	2005 GP2 CHAMPION,
	2002 FORMULA BMW CHAMPION

CAREER HISTORY

Partnered by Lewis Hamilton through much of his karting career, this son of 1982 World Champion Keke Rosberg raced all over Europe and even in the USA, with finishing as runner-up in the European Formula A kart series behind Lewis in 2000 being a highlight. Nico's first foray into car racing was a major success as he won the 2002 Formula BMW ADAC series. Scoring a win in his first season in the European Formula Three series was notable, and he ranked fourth overall at his second attempt in 2004, one place ahead of Lewis. Nico then joined the highly-rated ART Grand Prix team for GP2 in 2005 and beat Heikki Kovalainen to the title at the final round in Bahrain and thus earned himself promotion to Formula One. This was with Williams and Nico had the audacity to take fastest lap on his debut, at Bahrain. Held back by machinery not as competitive as some of his rivals, Nico produced his finest result so far, fourth, in the final race of 2007, in Brazil.

KAZUKI NAKAJIMA

He's the latest in a line of second generation Formula One racers, as son of Satoru, but he has already earned more fame by knocking over his pitcrew on his grand prix debut last October. Watch out, though, as he has raw speed aplenty.

Many Formula One fans might not have known much about Kazuki Nakajima when he made his grand debut in the final round, in Brazil. In many ways, with the three-way title battle overshadowing all else, some might not even have noticed that he had been promoted from his role as test driver to take the place of Alex Wurz who had announced his retirement. Well, apart from his too rapid arrival for his pitstop.

Indeed, younger fans might not even be aware of his father, Satoru, who clocked up 74 grands prix for Lotus then Tyrrell between 1987 and 1991, with a best finish of fourth place. But on the evidence of his performance in the race - he set the fifth fastest race lap en route to being 10th across the finish line - and his performances in GP2 through 2007 in which he ranked fifth overall, he has the speed.

Racing alongside Nico Rosberg in the season ahead, and under the tutelage of Sir Frank Williams and Patrick Head, Kazuki will hopefully rein in some of his more

Kazuki has the speed. All he needs now is a little more caution at his pit stops...

aggressive antics and fine tune his ability as Japan continues its search for a driver to take the country's first grand prix win.

That Williams is powered by Toyota engines and Kazuki is Japanese will not have escaped people's attention, and his signing will no doubt help the team's finances. In fact, it echoes what people said about his father when he arrived at Lotus when they had Honda engines, but Kazuki actually brings more than money, he brings youthful enthusiasm. Satoru was 34 when he reached Formula One, Kazuki turned 23 in January, so perhaps all that is similar is the red and white helmet livery. That he served as Williams' test and development driver through 2007 also means that he knows the team and the workings of the team already.

TRACK NOTES

Nationality:	JAPANESE
Born:	11 JANUARY, 1985, AICHI, JAPAN
Website:	WWW.KAZUKI-NAKAJIMA.COM
Teams:	WILLIAMS 2008

CAREER RECORD

First Grand Prix:	2007 BRAZILIAN GP
Grand Prix starts:	1
Grand Prix wins:	0
Poles:	0
Fastest laps:	0
Points:	0
Honours:	2005 JAPANESE FORMULA THREE RUNNER-UP, 2003 JAPANESE FORMULA TOYOTA CHAMPION

CAREER HISTORY

As soon as he turned 18, after six years of racing karts, Kazuki stepped up to Formula Toyota and showed his class by being crowned champion at the first attempt, immediately being snapped up by Toyota's driver development programme. Racing for TOM'S, the top team in Japanese Formula Three, he ranked fifth in 2004, then was runner-up behind his Brazilian team leader Joao Paulo de Oliveira the following year, also competing in the Japanese Super GT series. Satoru sent his son to try a year in the Formula Three Euro Series for Lewis Hamilton's old team, Manor Motorsport. Kazuki ranked seventh, with second place in the opening round his best result. He stayed in Europe for 2007 to race in GP2, and he beat team-mate Nicolas Lapierre, enjoying five straight podium finishes, with a best result of second behind Adam Carroll at the Hungaroring. He also tested for Williams, covering 4000 miles.

RED BULL RACING

The signs were there in the closing races of 2007 that the progress Red Bull Racing had been craving was finally beginning, bucking the team's trend of dropping away instead of advancing. For 2008, that first win remains the target.

Both drivers will want to experience more than flashes of speed.

Red Bull Racing: flash in the paddock or flash in the pan, that is the question. Well, everyone knows that they're flash in the paddock, their multi-levelled team building the heartbeat of every grand prix it attends. It's flamboyant, fun and free from the politics that sour the atmosphere in other team HQs. They have had two flashes in the pan with David Coulthard's third place at Monaco in 2006 and Mark Webber's similar result at the Nurburgring last year. For the considerable amount of money that Red Bull magnate Dietrich Mateschitz has thrown at the team since buying it from Jaguar Racing for the 2005 season, that's a poor return,

making it even more of a crying shame that Webber was taken out of second place in the rain in Japan last September by another Red Bull-liveried car. Fortunately for Coulthard, it wasn't him who did it, but Toro Rosso's Sebastian Vettel who triggered the double whammy.

However, that was then, and Red Bull had at least advanced to fifth overall, up from seventh in 2006. What counts, though, is where the team is heading in the months ahead, whether Newey's influence can be made to pay off with a car that is not only faster than its predecessors, but reliable too. This second point is vital, as the cars were parked up before the end of

PAST LEGENDS

This Milton Keynes-based team has had three different guises since it started life at Stewart Grand Prix in 1997, but British drivers have been the ones who delivered best in those. First off, Johnny Herbert gave Stewart its only grand prix win, in the European GP at the Nurburgring in 1999. He was outscored and usually outraced by team-mate Rubens Barrichello that year, but he was the one who came up trumps in a wild, wet-dry race. Herbert also raced for the team when it became Jaguar Racing in 2000. It was when the team turned green – on becoming Jaguar - that Northern Ireland's Eddie Irvine became the team leader and his pair of third-place finishes in 2001 gave the team a boost. However, it was the third of the British drivers, who raced in the third of the incarnations, who has scored the most points. This is David Coulthard, ironically a long-time protege of Stewart founder Jackie Stewart, who has raced for the team when it has been less than competitive as Red Bull, yet still come away with a podium finish at Monaco in 2006.

far too many races last year. Indeed, mechanical failures cost them valuable pre-season testing mileage as well. Should both targets be achieved, then, and only then, will Red Bull start to get serious, start to offer Coulthard and Webber the opportunity to offer any sort of championship challenge. With Ferrari and McLaren being so strong, Newey isn't predicting wins this year, though they would be nice.

Perhaps the most important move in seeking this firming up of their act was the appointment last summer of former Honda technical chief Geoff Willis as technical director, reporting to chief technical officer Newey. He is famed for solid engineering, something that the team clearly needs to be sure that manufacturing, quality control and packaging of all parts is improved. Particularly the

seamless gearbox, which often neutered the Renault engines that ought to have given the team a step up following its change from the Ferrari powerplants it used in 2006.

Former McLaren man Peter Prodromou leads the aerodynamics division and the RB4 will be the second car produced under chief designer Rob Marshall.

Coulthard and Webber firmed up their contract extensions for 2008 early on, but the Alonso factor last November made it look for a while as though the Spaniard would join this most well-funded of teams and the Australian would move on to Renault.

Webber is prized by the team for his qualifying expertise, although Coulthard matches him in the races, but both bring another skill that Newey values: the ability to sit down with the

engineers at the HQ and work through the cars' strengths and weaknesses, maximising their extensive experience.

Newey said last year that Red Bull's budget was only the seventh largest out of the 11 teams, which ought to dampen people's expectations, but the amount that Red Bull spends on

being flamboyant encourages onlookers to think that it must be more than that. Perhaps substance will move ahead of image in 2008, although that would certainly make the Formula One paddock a less exciting place to be, not that the Red Bull Racing drivers would be complaining.

FOR THE RECORD

Country of origin:	England
Team base:	Milton Keynes, England
Telephone:	(44) 1908 279700
Website:	WWW.REDBULLRACING.COM
Active in Formula One:	From 1997 (as Stewart until 2000 then Jaguar Racing until 2004)
Grands Prix contested:	188
Wins:	1
Pole positions:	1
Fastest laps:	0

2007 DRIVERS & RESULTS

Driver	Nationality	Races	Wins	Pts	Pos
David Coulthard	British	17	-	14	10th
Mark Webber	Australian	17	-	10	12th

THE TEAM

Chairman:	Dietrich Mateschitz
Team principal:	Christian Horner
Chief technical officer:	Adrian Newey
Technical director:	Geoff Willis
Head of race & test engineering:	Paul Monaghan
Chief designer:	Rob Marshall
Head of aerodynamics:	Peter Prodromou
Head of R&D:	Andrew Green
Team manager:	Jonathan Wheatley
Test driver:	tba
Chassis:	Red Bull RB4
Engine:	Renault V8
Tyres:	Bridgestone

Eddie Irvine raced for the team back when it was Jaguar Racing.

MARK WEBBER

There was a podium finish last year, at the Nurbrugring, but there should have been more. For Mark, the greatest gift for 2008 would be a car that contains all the speed you would expect from an Adrian Newey design allied to reliability.

One year ago, many questioned whether this ultra-competitive Australian had made the right choice in joining Red Bull Racing just as his former team, Williams, had landed works Toyota engines. The end of year tallies of 24 points for Red Bull and 33 for Williams suggest that he chose wrong. But it's this year, 2008, that will provide the true answer.

Examine the results of 2007 closely and both teams squandered good points scores through poor reliability. This is the area in which they must tidy up their act.

Examine Mark's speed in the car and he was the clear qualifying king in the Red Bull camp, outpacing team-mate David Coulthard (always more of a racer than a qualifier) 15 to two. His racing was super-strong too, and second place would most likely have come his way in the murk of Japan had Sebastian Vettel not slammed into him behind the safety car. A strong finish in the last race, Brazil, would have lifted the mood for the close-season, but fifth place went west when the engine and

Mark remains a qualifier supreme and deserves better reward for his application.

gearbox ceased to be connected.

So, there was speed for Mark to relish, and his nuggety drive to third place at the Nurburgring, but not much in the way of points. A good point, though, was the fact that the team became more competitive as the season wore on, reversing their previous trend of losing ground.

So, if Red Bull is indeed a team on the way up, we should look for Mark featuring right at the sharp end behind the Ferraris and McLarens, sniping for podium finishes and perhaps even more.

TRACK NOTES

Nationality:	AUSTRALIAN
Born:	27 AUGUST 1976, QUEANBEYAN, AUSTRALIA
Website:	WWW.MARKWEBBER.COM
Teams:	MINARDI 2002, JAGUAR 2003-2004, WILLIAMS 2005-2006, RED BULL RACING 2007-2008

CAREER RECORD

First Grand Prix:	2002 AUSTRALIAN GP
Grand Prix starts:	104
Grand Prix wins:	0
	best result: third, 2005 Monaco GP, 2007 European GP
Poles:	0
Fastest laps:	0
Points:	79
Honours:	2001 FORMULA 3000 RUNNER-UP, 1998 FIA GT RUNNER-UP, 1996 BRITISH FORMULA FORD RUNNER-UP & FORMULA FORD FESTIVAL WINNER

CAREER HISTORY

A spell in karting was followed by two years in Australian Formula Ford before he continued in the same category when he came to Britain in 1996. He ranked as runner-up and won the Formula Ford Festival. Helped by rugby legend David Campese, Mark advanced to British Formula Three in 1997 and won en route to ranking fourth. Here, the single-seater trail went cold as Mercedes signed him to race its sportscars for the next two years. Mark bounced back to race in Formula 3000, finishing as runner-up to Justin Wilson in 2001 when he also tested for Benetton. Mark made it into Formula One as a racer for Minardi in 2002, starting with fifth place in his home grand prix. Two seasons with Jaguar showed Mark's speed and the car's frailties before he joined Williams for 2005. His qualifying runs remained a strength, as it did when he moved to Red Bull.

DAVID COULTHARD

Last year was a holding year for David while Red Bull Racing attempted to produce a competitive car. It was frustrating, but David continued to show that he still has race craft in spades. Now he wants a fast car, perhaps for his swansong at the top level.

If all the ingredients can be knitted together and Adrian Newey and the design crew can craft a top-rank car, there would be few finer sights in 2008 than David standing atop a podium celebrating his 14th win.

Why so? Because he'd deserve it. Because his patience and effort deserves reward. Because it's never easy to have to go about your business in the midfield when you used to shoot for the stars at the front? And because David has played a major role in the transformation of Red Bull (once Stewart then Jaguar Racing, don't forget) into a competitive outfit. It was he, after all, who coaxed his old friend Newey to follow him from McLaren to Red Bull.

Team-mate Mark Webber wiped the floor with David in qualifying last year – 15 to two – but, to David's delight, he ended the year with more points, 14 to 10, thanks to fifth places in Spain and Germany followed by fourth in Japan. Both were frustrated by the number of times their cars failed to reach the finish, and both are drivers who

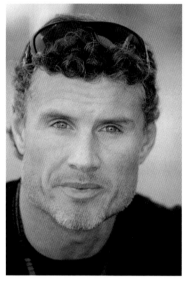

If the Red Bull RB4 proves to be any good, David will deliver, especially in the races.

must be relishing the rule change that has outlawed the use of traction control for 2008, as it will make the cars harder for rookies to jump into and get close to the

pace. David, like Mark, wants to maximise the value of his considerable experience, and rightly so. For, with his 37th birthday falling this March, David knows that the age police will be glancing his way if he fails.

TRACK NOTES

Nationality:	SCOTTISH
Born:	27 MARCH 1971, TWYNHOLM, SCOTLAND
Website:	WWW.DAVIDCOULTHARDF1.COM
Teams:	WILLIAMS 1994-1995, McLAREN 1996-2004, RED BULL 2005-2008

CAREER RECORD

First Grand Prix:	1994 SPANISH GP
Grand Prix starts:	229
Grand Prix wins:	13
	1995 Portuguese GP, 1997 Australian GP, Italian GP, 1998 San Marino GP, 1999 British GP, Belgian GP, 2000 British GP, Monaco GP, French GP, 2001 Brazilian GP, Austrian GP, 2002 Monaco GP, 2003 Australian GP
Poles:	12
Fastest laps:	18
Points:	527
Honours:	2001 FORMULA ONE RUNNER-UP, 1991 BRITISH FORMULA THREE RUNNER-UP & MACAU GP WINNER, 1989 McLAREN AUTOSPORT YOUNG DRIVER OF THE YEAR & BRITISH JUNIOR FORMULA FORD CHAMPION, 1988 SCOTTISH KART CHAMPION

CAREER HISTORY

Having won pretty much everything that he could in Scottish, and later British karting, David was an instant hit when he turned to cars in 1989. After Formula Ford, he stepped up to the GM Lotus Euroseries and gained useful knowledge of tracks that he'd visit later in his career. Rubens Barrichello pipped him to the 1991 British Formula Three crown. Two years in Formula 3000 followed before Ayrton Senna's death early in 1994 promoted David from Williams' test team to its race team alongside Damon Hill. He took his first win in Portugal in 1995, then moved to McLaren – the team that had awarded him a run in one of its cars at the end of his first car racing season – starting a nine-year relationship that yielded a further 12 wins but no titles, as Michael Schumacher dominated before he moved to Red Bull Racing for 2005. Wins haven't been on offer since, but David used his wise head and strong race craft to finish third at Monaco in 2006.

TOYOTA

Toyota has the money to succeed, but does it have the will? After six years in Formula One, few are any the wiser as this team shuns the accepted approach and tries to take on a thinking-on-their-feet team with a corporate management style.

Both drivers were frustrated in 2007 and the team needs to respond.

The world would be a very boring place if everyone looked the same, acted the same and achieved the same. But Toyota continues to pursue glory in Formula One in a manner that is so counter the success of the great teams that it beggars belief. Sure, Ferrari, McLaren, Williams and Renault employ a large number of people, but their management structure is lean, all answerable to the person at the top of the team. What does Toyota do? It answers to the person at the top of the automotive giant rather than the top of the team. It rules through consensus and committee. Does it work? No.

So, despite showing promise in its fourth year of Formula One, 2005, this Japanese giant is only making up the numbers, padding out the midfield. With a budget as massive as theirs, it's unforgivable.

The blame can't be laid squarely on the shoulders of the drivers, as both Jarno Trulli and Ralf Schumacher have won grands prix. No, the team has simply been too safe and too conservative – as you would expect from a committee – and it has said that it plans to adopt a more aggressive approach in the way with which it designs its cars for 2008 and beyond. And so it will have to do if it is to elevate itself from being only the seventh fastest team of the

PAST LEGENDS

Toyota has yet to hit the heights since it broke into Formula One in 2002. However, had they stuck with their first-year drivers – Mika Salo and Allan McNish – they might have benefitted from continuity that could have helped them forward in 2003 rather than starting afresh with two new drivers. Salo did score points on Toyota's debut in Australia, but this was a grand prix that no-one appeared to want to finish. Perhaps the Toyota hierarchy will point to the fact that their replacement of this pair with Cristiano da Matta and Olivier Panis for 2003 was a success as it resulted in Toyota running first and second in the British GP. However, this was chiefly down to the team producing a much more competitive car and also both cars pitting early before the bulk of the field at Silverstone dived into the pits when a safety car was deployed after a protester ran onto the circuit. In truth, though, the fact that Ralf Schumacher and Jarno Trulli – grand prix winners both – joined Toyota showed how much progress they reckoned that the team would make. Would, but hasn't as yet...

11 teams competing last year.

To achieve the required step forward, and shoot for the podium finishes that remain the team's goal, Toyota has beefed up its aerodynamics department to make this year's car more aero efficient. Head of department Mark Gillan is confident that the TF108 will be a step forward, but this will only be acheived if he and senior general manager of chassis Pascal Vasselon have been given a free hand. It will be judged on its relative speed at the opening race in Australia.

Apart from being neither faster nor reliable, one of the problems last year was that the drivers almost inevitably made dreadful starts as the TF107's launch control was less than sparkling and undid in particular Trulli's excellent qualifying efforts. That each driver peaked with a sixth place finish emphasises how far behind the top three of Ferrari, McLaren and BMW Sauber they were operating, managing only to pick up the scraps off the top table when the trio tripped up. Poor reliability hit Toyota hard.

While Schumacher has parted company with the team, Trulli has been kept on, but he is under no illusion that he may not see out his contract that is through to the end of 2009 as neither team president John Howett - supported at the head of the team this year by Tadashi Yamashina - nor anyone else at the team was prepared last autumn to say that any contract was safe. Team representatives even added that they would no longer sign long-term driver contracts. Well, that's certainly one way to keep its drivers on their toes.

Joining Trulli in the driver line-up this year is Timo Glock, a young gun to provide some youthful impetus, and both will be helped big time if Toyota improves the reliability of its cars. The banning of driver aids ought to cancel out the infuriating two to three place loss at the starts too, which should certainly cheer up Trulli.

Olivier Panis raced for Toyota in 2003 and starred in the British GP.

FOR THE RECORD

Country of origin:	Germany
Team base:	Cologne, Germany
Telephone:	(49) 2234 1823444
Website:	WWW.TOYOTA-F1.COM
Active in Formula One:	From 2002
Grands Prix contested:	105
Wins:	0
Pole positions:	2
Fastest laps:	1

2007 DRIVERS & RESULTS

Driver	Nationality	Races	Wins	Pts	Pos
Ralf Schumacher	German	17	-	5	16th
Jarno Trulli	Italian	17	-	8	13th

THE TEAM

Chairman & team principal:	Tadashi Yamashina
President:	John Howett
Executive vice-president:	Yoshiaki Kinoshita
General manager, engine:	Luca Marmorini
General manager, chassis:	Pascal Vasselon
Technical co-ordinator:	Noritoshi Arai
Chief engineer:	Dieter Gass
Head of aerodynamics:	Mark Gillan
Team manager:	Richard Cregan
Test driver:	Kamui Kobayashi
Chassis:	Toyota TF108
Engine:	Toyota V8
Tyres:	Bridgestone

JARNO TRULLI

As one of many drivers who finished 2007 less than happy with their results, Jarno has been considered fortunate by some to keep his drive with Toyota for 2008. However, if Toyota can progress, he'll stick it high up on the grid.

If you swim, you swim. You don't want to tread water, yet this is what Toyota's mediocrity inflicted on Jarno and team-mate Ralf Schumacher last year. On the strength of his performances in qualifying, Jarno stays on while Ralf has been dropped. Mind you, even with a contract through until the end of 2009 the Italian's retention of his seat was in doubt as the season came to a close, and he was mentioned in connection with a move to Force India F1, the team formerly known as Spyker for whom he drove when it was in its original iteration as Jordan.

This is not a pleasant position for a driver of Jarno's merit to be stewing in, with all his excellence in qualifying inevitably being undermined by the regular slide back down the order from the tail of the top 10 once the race got underway.

Add to this the fact that Toyota also slid down the order, losing ground to the other midfield teams through the year, and you can imagine how dispiriting it was for

Jarno's talents have been insufficiently rewarded through his Formula One career.

Jarno as the seventh places he picked up in the early-season races at Sepang and Sakhir could be added to only by sixth place at Indianapolis in June and then nothing until a point for eighth in the final race in Brazil at the end of October.

Jarno has one of the best brains in Formula One and he's going to need all of its powers of analysis to help Toyota out of the mess it has painted itself into with its desire not to fail rather than its lust to win making it way too conservative in its design choices, thus consigning it to a level of mediocrity that a driver of Jarno's talents doesn't deserve. In fact, it could finish his career.

TRACK NOTES

Nationality:	ITALIAN
Born:	13 JULY 1974, PESCARA, ITALY
Website:	WWW.JARNOTRULLI.COM
Teams:	MINARDI 1997, PROST 1997-1999, JORDAN 2000-2001, RENAULT 2002-2004, TOYOTA 2005-2008

CAREER RECORD	
First Grand Prix:	1997 AUSTRALIAN GP
Grand Prix starts:	184
Grand Prix wins:	1
	2004 Monaco GP
Poles:	3
Fastest laps:	0
Points:	183
Honours:	1996 GERMAN FORMULA THREE CHAMPION, 1994 WORLD KART CHAMPION

CAREER HISTORY

A world karting champion in the 100FK class as long ago as 1991, Jarno was the one to beat in the mid-1990s, ending up with the 125KC world karting title in 1995, by which time he had been propelled straight into Formula Three midway through the season by Flavio Briatore and won the final two German rounds ahead of Ralf Schumacher. He stayed on for a full German Formula Three campaign in 1996 and was a clear champion, with Heidfeld third. Deciding there was no time to waste, Jarno set his sights on Formula One and a late deal led to him racing for Minardi in 1997. Midway through the year, he was transferred to Prost to cover for the injured Olivier Panis and duly led much of the Austrian GP. After finishing second in the 1999 European GP, Jarno moved to Jordan, then on to Renault in 2002. After flurries of promise and numerous disappointments, he landed his so far only win, at Monaco in 2004, later quitting Renault for Toyota.

TIMO GLOCK

This is Timo's second crack at Formula One - the first came with Jordan in 2004 - and this time he is expected to reveal his true class. Whether that will be in the midfield or in the leading pack depends on the car Toyota that puts beneath him.

It seemed to be this 25-year-old German's destiny last year to be champion in Formula One's feeder formula, GP2, but everything possible seemed to transpire against it, with one of the most ridiculous moments coming at the race supporting the French GP when he and his iSport team-mate Andreas Zuber clashed when accelerating away from the front row of the grid, both being eliminated on the spot. There were mechanical woes through the season too. However, Timo was too good to fail and wrapped up the title ahead of Lucas di Grassi at the final round.

So, Formula One beckoned. Actually, that should that say beckoned again, for Timo had four outings with Jordan in 2004, even finishing in seventh place on his debut in Canada, before losing his ride and having to regain his career momentum via a spell in Champ Cars in 2005 then two years of GP2.

To make it to the pinnacle twice is quite an achievement, as there can be just as

Timo certainly deserves a second crack at motor racing's most senior category.

many pitfalls second time around or even the bad luck to have a shooting star as a contemporary, as he did with Lewis Hamilton in GP2 in 2006.

Just to prove that nothing appears to come easily to Timo, he then found himself caught between two teams last autumn, as both BMW Sauber, for whom he was the Friday test driver last year, and Toyota claimed to have him under contract. Eventually, in mid-November, the Contracts Recognition Board said he was free to race for Toyota as team-mate to Jarno Trulli.

Formula One needs solid, intelligent drivers graduating to its ranks and the wealth of experience, including experience of adversity, can only stand him in good stead for the challenges ahead.

TRACK NOTES

Nationality:	GERMAN
Born:	18 MARCH, 1982, LINDENFELS, GERMANY
Website:	WWW.TIMO-GLOCK.DE
Teams:	JORDAN 2004, TOYOTA 2008

CAREER RECORD

First Grand Prix:	2004 CANADIAN GP
Grand Prix starts:	4
Grand Prix wins:	0
Poles:	0
Fastest laps:	0
Points:	0
Honours:	2007 GP2 CHAMPION,
	2001 GERMAN FORMULA BMW CHAMPION, 2000
	GERMAN FORMULA BMW JUNIOR CHAMPION

CAREER HISTORY

After karting, Timo stepped up to cars in 1990 and promptly won the BMW ADAC Formula Junior Cup. He won the German Formula BMW title in 2001, beating Christian Klien. Timo then had two strong years in Formula Three before reaching Formula One in 2004, with Jordan as a replacement for Giorgio Pantano. Despite finishing seventh on that debut in Canada, he had to wait until the end of the year for three more outings when Pantano was dropped. Sadly, these didn't keep him in a drive and so 2005 was spent racing in Champ Car for the Rocketsports team. He ended as easily the top rookie, ranking eighth overall. Anxious to get back to Formula One, he returned to Europe to race in GP2 in 2006, ranking fourth as Lewis Hamilton blitzed the championship. Clearly the class of the GP2 field in 2007, anything that could go wrong did and it was only at the final round that Timo claimed the crown.

TORO ROSSO

Fourth place in China last year might be a sign of things to come, so Toro Rosso can look forward to the best year that this team that was once Minardi has ever had. In Vettel and Bourdais, it has drivers of talent but minimal experience.

Vitantonio Liuzzi fought hard, but the team dropped him for 2008.

In truth, the link with perennial tailenders Minardi, as the team was until the end of 2005, is all but irrelevant now as Ferrari engines and chassis remarkably similar to those raced by their midfield sister team, Red Bull Racing, have propelled Toro Rosso up the order.

The highlight of 2007 was most certainly Sebastian Vettel's amazing run to fourth place at the penultimate race in China. It was no fluke, though, as the German rookie had been running third in the previous race, in the wet in Japan, until a little faux pas behind the safety car when he took out himself and Red Bull Racing's Mark Webber who was running second in an incident

that certainly caused some waves on the pond.

However, it was the overall improvement of every element of the team that offers encouragement, and much of this is down to money from Red Bull. Certainly, former team owner Paul Stoddart would have loved to be able to shape his team of old with similar largesse. The team numbers 150 people, so it's way up on its Minardi days. Conversely, sister team Red Bull Racing employs more than 500, with a similar discrepancy in the amount of testing they do.

Talking of money, rumours circulated the paddock last year that Toro Rosso was up for sale,

PAST LEGENDS

By the end of its first season, 2007, Scuderia Toro Rosso has employed just three drivers - Vitantonio Liuzzi, Scott Speed and Sebastian Vettel. However, all three were racing for a team with a budget far greater than anything their predecessors enjoyed when the team raced as Minardi through 21 seasons between 1985 and 2005. It was a team that proved the way into Formula One for the likes of Giancarlo Fisichella, Jarno Trulli, Mark Webber and Fernando Alonso, and even the way out for the veteran Michele Alboreto. However, the driver who stands out for Minardi is the one who not only scored the most points - 16 - and raced for it the most times - 102 - but also gave it its best ever grid position: Pierluigi Martini. His first spell with the Italian team in 1985 was weak and he missed two years before he made it back to Formula One, with Minardi. His day of days came at the United States GP at Phoenix in 1990 when he made the most of his Pirelli qualifiying tyres and qualified second alongside Ayrton Senna. Senna won, Martini fell to seventh, although he did twice finish fourth.

with Nicolas Todt - son of the Ferrari team boss - said to be keen to step up from running a team in GP2, with backing from a Bahraini business consortium. However, no deal had been done by the end of 2007, leaving former grand prix winner Gerhard Berger as the man in control and Franz Tost as the hands-on team principal.

It wasn't all sweetness and light as Toro Rosso worked its way towards a career-topping seventh overall, though, as neither Vitantonio Liuzzi nor team-mate Scott Speed were kept on for 2008. Indeed, Speed was fired after insubordination in a major flare-up with Tost after the American had crashed out of the European GP at the Nurburgring. His replacement, Vettel, enjoyed that was growing better by the race and delivered the goods.

Liuzzi did all he could, and collected sixth place in China, making it a bumper day for Toro Rosso, but his place has been filled by four-time Champ Car champion Sebastien Bourdais, a driver destined for Formula One half a decade ago but unable to land a drive then and thus headed to the USA to further his career. He brings plenty of F1 testing experience, though, so don't think of the French ace as a rookie.

Technical director Giorgio Ascanelli joined last April, taking over from Alex Hitzinger, and the drivers were raving about some of the development parts that his design team introduced for the final races of last year. The whole element of improvement through a season, and fighting at a higher level than before has fired up the Minardi crew of old and they are enjoying the experience. So, it's safe to say that all at Toro Rosso have high hopes for the season ahead. But, they must be aware that it won't do to beat Dietrich Mateschitz's main team, Red Bull Racing.

FOR THE RECORD

Country of origin:	Italy
Team base:	Faenza, Italy
Telephone:	(39) 546 696111
Website:	WWW.SCUDERIATORORSSO.COM
Active in Formula One:	From 1985 (as Minardi until 2006)
Grands Prix contested:	376
Wins:	0
Pole positions:	0
Fastest laps:	0

2007 DRIVERS & RESULTS

Driver	Nationality	Races	Wins	Pts	Pos
Vitantonio Liuzzi	Italian	17	-	3	18th
Scott Speed	American	10	-	-	n/a
Sebastian Vettel	German	17	-	5	14th

THE TEAM

Team owners:	Dietrich Mateschitz & Gerhard Berger
Team principal:	Franz Tost
General manager:	Gianfranco Fantuzzi
Technical director:	Giorgio Ascanelli
Chief engineer:	Laurent Mekies
Team manager:	Massimo Rivola
Technical co-ordinator:	Sandro Parrini
Test driver:	tba
Chassis:	Scuderia Toro Rosso STR3
Engine:	Ferrari V8
Tyres:	Bridgestone

Pierluigi Martini starts his Minardi on the front row at Phoenix in '90.

SEBASTIAN VETTEL

It's safe to say that this 20-year-old German had a year of highs and lows in 2007, from losing his regular Friday runs at grands prix for BMW Sauber to joining Toro Rosso to taking Mark Webber out of the Japanese GP to finishing fourth in China.

Type German and racing hot shot into an internet search engine and it will probably produce the name of Sebastian Vettel. If it doesn't, it ought to, as he has the look of a future star.

As always with Formula One, a driver can be the most talented in the world but if a seat isn't available that talent might wither away. Smily-faced Sebastian doesn't have to worry about that fate that has led to so many hotshots sliding back into oblivion, for his foot is in the Formula One door.

BMW Sauber helped him try Formula One for size and then Scott Speed's premature departure from Toro Rosso last year with seven grands prix remaining was an opportunity too good to miss. Here was a Red Bull-sponsored team and he was already a Red Bull-sponsored driver. Snap!

The fact that he's suitably irreverent, with a welcome sense of fun, has already made him popular in the paddock and with his team. But what really cheers his mechanics is the fact that he can really

Sebastian made quite a splash in last year's closing races, suggesting great promise.

drive. Yes, there was the blot on the copybook at the Japanese GP when he was running third - a giddyingly high position for a rookie and even more so for someone

at the wheel of a Toro Rosso - and took out Red Bull's Mark Webber ahead of him.

To bounce back from that and all the criticism that came his way was one thing. But to do so and then finish fourth at the next race on merit - well, promoted one place by Hamilton's trip into the Shanghai gravel - was quite another.

Already the youngest point-scorer in Formula One history, Sebastian is a driver who could have a very big future.

TRACK NOTES

Nationality:	GERMAN
Born:	3 JULY, 1987, HEEPENHEIM, GERMANY
Website:	WWW.SEBASTIANVETTEL.DE
Teams:	BMW SAUBER 2007, TORO ROSSO 2007-2008

CAREER RECORD

First Grand Prix:	2007 UNITED STATES GP
Grand Prix starts:	17
Grand Prix wins:	0
	best result: 4th 2007 Chinese GP
Poles:	0
Fastest laps:	0
Points:	6

Honours: 2006 EUROPEAN FORMULA 3 RUNNER-UP, 2004 GERMAN FORMULA BMW CHAMPION, 2003 GERMAN FORMULA BMW RUNNER-UP, 2001 EUROPEAN & GERMAN JUNIOR KART CHAMPION

CAREER HISTORY

The young Sebastian was a major player in karts. He won the European junior title in 2001 and the German one, plus the Monaco junior kart cup. He finished as runner-up in the Formula BMW ADAC Championship when he moved up to cars in 2003, aged 16, and he blitzed the opposition to win that series in 2004, taking 18 wins from 20 races. After finishing fifth in European Formula Three in 2005, as top rookie, Sebastian enjoyed his first Formula One run-out, with BMW Sauber at Jerez. staying on in European Formula Three, Sebastian was pipped to the crown, but was given a more intense taste of Formula One by becoming the third driver for BMW Sauber. Holding down that same position for 2007, he also raced in World Series by Renault, winning at the Nurburgring before landing a full-time Formula One ride with Toro Rosso after scoring points on a one-off ride with BMW Sauber as stand-in for the injured Robert Kubica in the US GP.

SEBASTIEN BOURDAIS

It seemed as though Formula One had passed him by, but Sebastien Bourdais - a four-time Champ Car champ - has made the leap and will be back racing against the contemporaries that he raced against and beat before heading to the USA.

Sebastien used to wear spectacles with red frames that made him look a bit like children's TV character Joe 90. Once in the cockpit, though, there's no mistaking his forceful attack and sheer speed.

Just look at his career record. For anyone who is good enough to be a Formula 3000 champion deserves respect, for this was the all-but exclusive feeder formula in the days before a host of powerful slicks-and-wings categories cluttered the market between Formula Three and the pinnacle of Formula One. So, in theory, the Formula 3000 champion was the heir apparent, the pick of the pack looking to become grand prix drivers. Back in 2002, he beat Giorgio Pantano and Antonio Pizzonia. Undeniably, they have failed to shine at the very top, but Sebastien's inability to find a race seat in Formula One for 2003 led to a decision to try his luck in the States. Undoubtedly, the Champ Car series is on the slide, but four titles tell you all you need to know: he is a winner.

Sebastien willhave to adapt from his success in Champ Cars to Formula One.

For 2008, though, Sebastien will be in the strange position of having to learn from a rookie, as team-mate Sebastian Vettel has the headstart of racing for Scuderia Toro Rosso in the final seven races of 2007, so is bedded into the team.

Sebastien will also have to learn tracks, but Champ Car drivers have to do that most years as that series moves to pastures new, so he should be fine on that count, with his worldly experience also a welcome addition to the team.

The biggest shock of all for this genial Frenchman will probably just how dog-eat-dog the Formula One environment can be, especially if Vettel outpaces him.

TRACK NOTES

Nationality:	FRENCH
Born:	28 FEBRUARY, 1979, LE MANS, FRANCE
Website:	WWW.SEBASTIEN-BOURDAIS.COM
Teams:	TORO ROSSO 2008

CAREER RECORD	
First Grand Prix:	2008 AUSTRALIAN GP
Grand Prix starts:	0
Grand Prix wins:	0
Poles:	0
Fastest laps:	0
Points:	0
Honours:	2004, 2005, 2006 & 2007 CHAMPCAR CHAMPION, 2002 FORMULA 3000 CHAMPION, 1999 FRENCH FORMULA 3 CHAMPION, 1997 FRENCH FORMULA RENAULT RUNNER-UP

CAREER HISTORY

Born in Le Mans and the son of a racing father, Patrick, it was always likely that Sebastien would go racing, and this he did. Runner-up in the French Formula Renault series at his second attempt in 1997, Sebastien also took two bites at the cherry in Formula Three, becoming French champion in 1999. Formula 3000 was next and it took until 2002 to win this title with Super Nova Racing by outpointing Giorgio Pantano, racing sportscars on his spare weekends. But no ride was available in Formula One, so Sebastien headed to North America, for a regular ride in Champ Cars backed up by occasional Formula One test outings for Renault. Ranked fourth in his first year of Champ Cars with the crack Newman/Haas Racing team, scoring three wins, Sebastien then rattled off 27 more wins and four straight Champ Car titles through until the end of 2007, by which time his move to Formula One with Scuderia Toro Rosso had been confirmed.

HONDA RACING

Hit harder than most by the change from Michelins to Bridgestones as they took an aerodynamic route that didn't work, Honda were nowhere. Questions will be asked if they don't re-establish themselves and save Jenson Button's career.

It's safe to say that Honda gave Jenson Button a rough ride in 2007.

Honda really needs a great, competitive season in 2008, because ending up with egg on your face two seasons in a row is the sort of result that would convince the company's money men to seek termination, especially if fellow Japanese manufacturers Toyota was to come good and trounce them. Small wonder, then, that Honda was on a massive recruitment drive through 2007, particularly in the aerodynamics department.

In has come John Owen from BMW Sauber as senior aerodynamicist. Jorg Zander joined as deputy technical director, reporting to Shuhei Nakamoto, at the end of last season, followed by Loic Bigois

who filled the role of Honda Racing's head of aerodynamics from last December in place of Mariano Alperin-Bruvera. With the lengthy design lead time for today's Formula One cars, it will be Honda's 2009 challenger that might be the first to truly bare the new design team's mark.

However, the most important appointment of all came last November when Ross Brawn was coaxed back into action after a year's sabbatical and persuaded to join Honda rather than return to Ferrari. Certainly the best combination of technical brain and race strategist in the pit lane, he if anyone will put this team back on track.

It doesn't take much

PAST LEGENDS

John Surtees was a seven-time world champion on motorcycles and had become the first man to win the title on four wheels as well when he quit Ferrari for Honda in 1966. He didn't give Honda its first grand prix win – that was American Richie Ginther in Mexico in 1965 – but he guided Honda to its second, at Monza in 1967. His influence extended further than what he did in the cockpit, however, as it was his engineering nous that convinced Honda to commission Lola to build a chassis to replace its own, overweight offering. The team closed its doors at the end of 1968 and only re-emerged when Honda gradually bought its way into British American Racing, a team that had made its debut in 1999 having been built around Jacques Villeneuve. He left in 2003, just as BAR started to find its way and it was to another British driver, Jenson Button, that Honda turned to in its quest for glory. He had been close to victory several times when the team was still BAR, but his and Honda's day of days came at Hungary in 2006 when they triumphed together.

examination of the team's 2007 results to realise that this wasn't the outcome you'd expect of a well-funded team, especially with drivers of the calibre of Rubens Barrichello and Jenson Button. Just six points were scored, leaving the team eighth overall (ninth until McLaren's expulsion from the championship) and able to pull ahead of the little Super Aguri Racing team to which it supplies engines only at the 16th of the 17 grands prix.

In fact, 2007 will probably be recalled first and foremost for Honda's world livery.

It had all looked so good for Honda at the end of 2006, when the team was right on the pace at the final round. Their tally of 86 points put them fourth overall, not that far behind McLaren but well clear of BMW Sauber. Within a month, all high hopes for 2007 were dashed. This was when Honda tried Bridgestone tyres

for the first time and found they had lost all that they had gained and more. In short, the aerodynamic effect of the tyres on the car was a shock and proved that the RA107's aero concept had been developed in the wrong direction, a problem caused by starting the design of the car four months before the data about the 2007 tyres was released. With the tyres proving particularly different in the way that they deformed under heavy loads, there was excessive instability under braking.

On top of that, when Honda's new wind tunnel came on stream mid-season, it hadn't been calibrated properly, with understandably disappointing results.

For 2008, the team also intends to utilise CFD (Computational Fluid Dynamics) more to achieve the end goal of a fast and efficient car.

The driver line-up remains

the same for a third season, with Button earning particular praise last year for his cheer and diligence in the face of adversity, and further accolades for finishing fifth in the penultimate race, in China. Barrichello failed to score a single point and knows that this

will be his last year of Formula One if he doesn't deliver.

Even finishing in the top 10 was something of a triumph last year. This year, that will be expected at every race. Should Honda-engined Super Aguri outpoint them, swords will have to be fallen upon.

FOR THE RECORD

Country of origin:	England
Team base:	Brackley, England
Telephone:	(44) 01280 844000
Website:	WWW.HONDARACINGF1.COM
Active in Formula One:	From 1999 (as BAR)
Grands Prix contested:	153
Wins:	1
Pole positions:	3
Fastest laps:	0

2007 DRIVERS & RESULTS

Driver	Nationality	Races	Wins	Pts	Pos
Rubens Barrichello	Brazilian	17	-	-	n/a
Jenson Button	British	17	-	6	15th

THE TEAM

Chairman:	Yasuhiro Wada
Team principal:	Ross Brawn
Chief executive officer:	Nick Fry
Senior technical director:	Shuhei Nakamoto
Deputy technical director:	Jorg Zander
Engineering director:	Jacky Eeckelaert
Operations director:	Gary Savage
Chief designer:	Kevin Taylor
Head of aerodynamics:	Loic Bigois
Chief engineer:	Craig Wilson
Sporting director:	Ron Meadows
Test driver:	tba
Chassis:	RA108
Engine:	Honda V8
Tyres:	Bridgestone

Jacques Villeneuve battled when the team started life as BAR.

JENSON BUTTON

That Jenson was still able to smile last year was testament to his resilience and character. Honda had plunged from being fast in pre-season testing to being dreadful. If his smile is not more natural in 2008, he'll look elsewhere for a ride.

Jenson said even before last season was over that he was confident for 2008. Well, it was unlikely that Honda could have fared much worse than it did in 2007 when it only outscored its (considerably) junior team, Super Aguri. The area of transformation, he said, was going to be coming from the revamped aero department.

Think about it: Jenson gave Honda its first win in its modern incarnation in the 2006 Hungarian GP. He then rounded out the season with a competitive third place in Brazil. And then, nothing...

Finishing 15th in the 2007 season-opener in Australia was the reality check. It wasn't flukily bad either, as 12th place next time out was to prove. In fact, it took until the eighth round to break into the top 10, with eighth at Magny-Cours. Jenson reckoned this was the result of Honda's designers having gone down an aerodynamic cul-de-sac midway through 2006 that meant that team had to throw more downforce than

Jenson doesn't expect race wins this year, but some progress would be most welcome.

would have been ideal onto the front of the car. It wasn't an instant fix by any stretch of the imagination, with Jenson's fifth place

in the penultimate race in China the result more of his ability in mixed conditions.

Nigel Mansell said last year that Jenson "will never make it as a top-line Formula One driver". Given the equipment, though, few doubt that he will prove the 1992 world champion wrong.

TRACK NOTES

Nationality:	BRITISH
Born:	19 JANUARY 1980, FROME, ENGLAND
Website:	WWW.JENSONBUTTON.COM
Teams:	WILLIAMS 2000,
	BENETTON/RENAULT 2001-2002,
	BAR/HONDA 2003-2008

CAREER RECORD	
First Grand Prix:	2000 AUSTRALIAN GP
Grand Prix starts:	136
Grand Prix wins:	1
	2006 Hungarian GP
Poles:	3
Fastest laps:	0
Points:	229
Honours:	1999 MACAU FORMULA
	THREE RUNNER-UP, 1998 FORMULA FORD
	FESTIVAL WINNER, BRITISH FORMULA FORD
	CHAMPION & McLAREN AUTOSPORT BRDC
	YOUNG DRIVER, 1997 EUROPEAN SUPER A
	KART CHAMPION, 1991 BRITISH CADET
	KART CHAMPION

CAREER HISTORY

Jenson was 11 when he won his first British kart title, in the cadet class, but he had many more titles to his name in Europe and even winning the Ayrton Senna Memorial Cup at Suzuka, before stepping up to cars in 1988. He hit hard, winning the British title and the Formula Ford Festival, marking himself out as something special. Jenson then leapt straight to Formula Three, starting his first race from pole and ending the year third overall. It was while deciding to stay for a second year in Formula Three that the offer of a test run for Prost was proposed. He impressed so much that he was invited for a shoot-out with Bruno Junqueira to lands the second Williams seat for 2000. This he won and his skill was clear to see, developing through that season alongside Ralf Schumacher. A spell with Benetton and Renault didn't yield fruit, but BAR Honda did and he was often bettered only by Michael Schumacher. Finally, he struck gold in Hungary in 2006, before the team lost its competitive edge.

RUBENS BARRICHELLO

There was talk before last year's finale that it would be Rubens' last grand prix, but he has held on and Honda is honouring his contract. No-one can be more delighted to be reunited with a former colleague than Rubens with Ross Brawn.

Rubens was the baby of the Formula One paddock when he burst onto the scene with Jordan as a 20-year-old in 1993 and promptly ran behind only Ayrton Senna at Donington Park. But this now seems a very long time ago, with his lofty hairline making him look older than his 35 years and his status in the paddock is firmly as one of the old hands.

It seemed too, after a pointless second season with Honda in 2007 that his time was up. Rubens had a contract in hand for 2008, but last autumn it was far from certain that he would be kept on. there was even talk that he would be transferred to Super Aguri Racing, effectively Honda's B-team.

Sure, Rubens could have been paid off and headed home to Brazil to spend time with his beloved family, but his love is racing and he held on, delighted by former Ferrari colleague Ross Brawn being signed as team principal, a man to give Honda the direction it so clearly lacked last year.

In short, Rubens' 15-year Formula One

Rubens will be hoping that old friend Ross Brawn can put his career back on track.

career record with its tally of nine wins shows that he can fly given a good car – don't forget that he would occasionally outpace one Michael Schumacher when they were teamed together at Ferrari – and

not even his fiercest critic would say that he had one of those under him in 2007. It was unpredictable and unstable. Frustratingly for Rubens, the aerodynamic changes made through the year failed to get to the bottom of the RA107's inherent imbalance until the very end. Ninth place in the British GP was to stand as his best result.

So, things can only get better.

TRACK NOTES

Nationality:	BRAZILIAN
Born:	23 MAY 1972, SAO PAULO, BRAZIL
Website:	WWW.BARRICHELLO.COM.BR
Teams:	JORDAN 1993-1996, STEWART 1997-1999, FERRARI 2000-2005, HONDA 2006-2008

CAREER RECORD

First Grand Prix:	1993 SOUTH AFRICAN GP
Grand Prix starts:	252
Grand Prix wins:	9
2000 German GP, 2002 European GP, Hungarian GP, Italian GP, US GP, 2003 British GP, Japanese GP, 2004 Italian GP, Chinese GP	
Poles:	13
Fastest laps:	15
Points:	519
Honours:	2002 FORMULA ONE RUNNER-UP, 1991 BRITISH FORMULA THREE CHAMPION, 1990 EUROPEAN FORMULA OPEL CHAMPION, 1988 BRAZILIAN KART CHAMPION

CAREER HISTORY

With his family home overlooking Interlagos, Rubens was always likely to race. He was quick too and had the Brazilian karting title and a little Formula Ford experience under his belt before, backed by a consortium of businessmen, he headed for Europe before his 18th birthday. He won the European Formula Opel series, then backed that up with the British Formula Three title in 1991. Formula Rubens ranked third in Formula 3000 and Formula One beckoned for 1993 and he amazed onlookers when he ran second in only his third grand prix for Jordan, at Donington, before his car failed. He finished second for Jordan, in Canada in 1995, then again for Stewart at Monaco in 1997 and also at the Nurburgring in 1999, but it took a move to Ferrari in 2000 for him to become a winner, landing his first at Hockenheim. After eight more wins, Rubens joined Honda for 2006.

SUPER AGURI

Honda would have been delighted that Super Aguri picked itself off the bottom of the grid in 2007, but it must have fretted that it took until the penultimate race to move ahead on points... It's hard to see such an upturn occurring again.

Anthony Davidson and Takuma Sato are looking for continued progress.

One of the most entertaining moments of the 2007 Formula One World Championship came at the opening round in Australia. Many will have missed it, but it came when former Formula One racer Aguri Suzuki's team exceeded its expectations in qualifying. They were delighted when both drivers avoided the elimination of the slowest six drivers and got through into the second qualifying session, but were then caught out when Takuma Sato made it through into qualifying three, for the top 10 drivers. The reason for their concern was that they had never expected to get that far and so had done only a few calculations on how best to fuel the car should they do so...

What was noticed, though, was the team's greatest moment to date when Sato raced to sixth place in the topsy-turvy Canadian Grand Prix and gave the team its moment of moments near the end when he overtook reigning world champion Fernando Alonso's McLaren fair and square. That proved what a remarkable journey this little team had been on from its 11th hour inception ahead of the 2006 season.

In fact, had one of the marmots that live on the Isle Notre Dame not run out in front of Anthony Davidson's sister car earlier in that same race, they might have come away with

PAST LEGENDS

There have only been five drivers who have raced for Super Aguri Racing through its first two years in Formula One, and Takuma Sato stands out as the most successful as the only point-scorer thus far. He claimed the team's first point with a strong run to eighth place in the Spanish GP in 2007 in the fourth race of the Japanese-financed team's second campaign. This he eclipsed with an extraordinary run to sixth place in Canada, even overtaking the McLaren of reigning world champion Fernando Alonso. Had it not been for an errant marsupial, the result could have been even better, as Anthony Davidson was heading for a likely fourth place in this jumbled race when a marmot ran into his path and bent his front wing. Thus far, the cast also includes Yuji Ide who struggled in the early part of Super Aguri's inaugural season as the team tried to find its feet with outdated equipment, as did Frenchman Franck Montagny when he took over. At least Sakon Yamamoto had a newer car to race, but it's safe to say that they were all kept in the shadows as the team settled in.

their first podium. A pit stop to change his mangled front wing tipped him down the order, added to by the fact that the team didn't know that he was coming in.

Off the back of this, and Sato's point for eighth in the Spanish GP, it's hard to know what to expect from the smallest team on the grid in the season ahead. What we do know is that, for the second season running, they will be campaigning ex-works Honda chassis. While this wasn't such a bad thing last year, as it was the 2006 Honda RA106 that it ran, the form of the Honda RA107 was far from glowing. As it happens, all might not be lost, as there was talk that Honda wouldn't be able to supply new chassis in time for the start of the season.

So, perhaps, we might have the situation in which Super Aguri outscores its parent team in the early races. Except the arrival of Ross Brawn at the helm at Honda ought to prevent that from being the case.

One of the greatest skills that Brawn brings to a team is organisation, and this is something that Super Aguri worked hard on last year. Feeling that they weren't communicating well on the pit wall, they moved all the engineers into one of the trucks and, first time out in Spain, were rewarded with the team's first ever point. The flip side was having no engineer on the pit wall in Canada to spot Davidson coming in. After that, there was always one engineer on the pit wall.

Knowing that they are unlikely to challenge the top teams, the team is prepared to take gambles that won't cost them the win, but could help them towards the points.

In short, though, the whole enterprise has been a gamble and Super Aguri were caught short last year when two sponsors defaulted, starting speculation that Aguri Suzuki might be bought out. At the time of writing, however, this has not happened.

Sato and Davidson are being kept on for 2008, with the British driver due some fortune in the races so that he can make the most of his superior qualifying form and maximise his ability to make a one-stop strategy work.

FOR THE RECORD

Country of origin:	England
Team base:	Witney, England
Telephone:	(44) 0993 871600
Website:	www.superaguri-f1.com
Active in Formula One:	From 2006
Grands Prix contested:	35
Wins:	0
Pole positions:	0
Fastest laps:	0

2007 DRIVERS & RESULTS

Driver	Nationality	Races	Wins	Pts	Pos
Anthony Davidson	British	17	-	-	n/a
Takuma Sato	Japanese	17	-	4	17th

THE TEAM

Team principal:	Aguri Suzuki
Managing director:	Daniele Audetto
Technical director:	Mark Preston
Sporting director:	Graham Taylor
Chief designer:	Peter McCool
Chief aerodynamicist:	Ben Wood
Head of R&D:	Gerry Hughes
Operations director:	Kevin Lee
Team manager:	Mick Ainsley-Cowlishaw
Test driver:	tba
Chassis:	Super Aguri SA08
Engine:	Honda V8
Tyres:	Bridgestone

The team's day of days came with sixth in the 2007 Canadian GP.

TAKUMA SATO

This smiling Japanese driver had reason to smile last year as Super Aguri made impressive strides in its second season, with this feisty driver enjoying his forays into the thick of the midfield action and most especially passing Alonso on merit.

Many successful sportspeople utilise the power of positive thoughts to drive them on and you can be sure that Takuma has locked into his mindset the moment late in the Canadian GP when he realised that he was catching Fernando Alonso. Yes, a driver who has never won a grand prix closing down a double world champion. Furthermore, a driver in a Super Aguri homing in on a McLaren. Surreal it might have felt, but very real it was and the subsequent passing manoeuvre led to Takuma claiming sixth place.

Not the best of qualifiers, Takuma proved again and again his attributes as a racer, and he'd already given the team its first ever point with eighth place on merit in the fourth round, in Spain.

Off the back of these performances, Takuma's stock continued to rise in Japan. Indeed, after his race in Barcelona, Toyota were reputed to be seeing whether they could sign him as a replacement for Ralf Schumacher for this year.

Takuma has matured enormously through having to fight for his Formula One career.

For 2008, though, Takuma knows that he has a serious rival if he is to remain as Japan's top driver as Kazuki Nakajima looks set to make a name for himself with the considerably more competitive Williams team and it's largely down to their respective teams to offer competitive cars to decide which will be the one who comes out on top.

What makes Takuma a delight to watch behind the wheel is that although he's small in stature, he's big in heart and his opening laps are usually something to behold. The European GP at the Nurburgring was a good example of this, as he overtook six rivals on the opening lap, in mixed conditions.

More please.

TRACK NOTES

Nationality:	JAPANESE
Born:	28 JANUARY, 1977, TOKYO, JAPAN
Website:	WWW.TAKUMASATO.COM
Teams:	JORDAN 2002, BAR 2003-2005,
	SUPER AGURI RACING 2006-2008

CAREER RECORD	
First Grand Prix:	2002 AUSTRALIAN GP
Grand Prix starts:	89
Grand Prix wins:	0
	best result: third 2004 US GP
Poles:	0
Fastest laps:	0
Points:	44
Honours:	2001 BRITISH FORMULA THREE
	CHAMPION

CAREER HISTORY

Unusual for bypassing karting, Takuma almost bypassed the Japanese junior formulae too by racing in Formula Vauxhall in Britain in 1998 then Formula Opel in Europe in 1999, ranking sixth despite switching to British Formula Three towards the end of the year. Back for a full campaign in 2000, Takuma ranked third overall for Carlin Motorsport. In 2001, Takuma added his name to the list of British Formula Three champions, pipping team-mate Anthony Davidson. Formula One was next, as Takuma joined Jordan thanks to the team running Honda engines. Two points were scored. The BAR team used him as its test driver in 2003 and he was rewarded with a race outing at the last race before a full campaign in 2004 in which he ranked eighth and stood on the podium at the US GP. His tally of just one point in 2005 was thus a disappointment and he was kicked out, only to have his career saved by the formation of Super Aguri.

ANTHONY DAVIDSON

Anthony was one of the stars of qualifying throughout the 2007 World Championship as Super Aguri advanced from the tail of the grid to the midfield. Matters may not be so easy in his second season with the Japanese team.

It's hard not to focus on the battle at the front and miss the sterling efforts of the drivers in the teams towards the back. However, the qualifying format with its three sessions and knock-out element redresses this. And Anthony Davidson must be thankful for this as almost all of his races bar the Canadian GP last year were in the anonymity of the hinterland.

What made people remember the stellar form he had displayed on grand prix Fridays in 2006 when he was the third Honda driver and often was fastest of all in the first practice session was his run to 11th place in qualifying for the Turkish GP. It humbled the performance of drivers in superior machinery and really boosted Anthony in the eyes of the people who count. By this stage of the season, he could have been sitting on the points from a good finish, perhaps fifth place, in the Canadian GP, but for the intercession of a marmot that wandered into the path of his Super Aguri and mangled its front wing. That

Anthony showed great speed in qualifying, but needs to have better luck in the races.

this problem was exacerbated by his crew not being ready for his unplanned pitstop meant that Anthony fell to an eventual 11th on a day when it could have been he rather than team-mate Takuma Sato who recorded the team's best ever result. Being taken out of the Hungarian GP by Giancarlo Fisichella was another disappointment and by year's end Anthony had failed to finish higher than 11th, something that he did three times. The speed was there, but the results weren't.

For 2008, Super Aguri will be equipped with last year's Honda, and this won't necessarily be a step forward from the 2006 Hondas the team used in 2007.

TRACK NOTES

Nationality:	BRITISH
Born:	18 APRIL 1979, HEMEL HEMPSTEAD, ENGLAND
Website:	WWW.ANTHONYDAVIDSON.COM
Teams:	MINARDI 2002, BAR 2005, SUPER AGURI 2007-2008

CAREER RECORD	
First Grand Prix:	2002 HUNGARIAN GP
Grand Prix starts:	20
Grand Prix wins:	0
Poles:	0
Fastest laps:	0
Points:	0
Honours:	2001 BRITISH FORMULA THREE RUNNER-UP, 2000 McLAREN AUTOSPORT BRDC WINNER & BRITISH FORMULA FORD RUNNER-UP, 1995 BRITISH JUNIOR KART CHAMPION

CAREER HISTORY

Blessed with the perfect physique for karting – short and light – Anthony was a hotshot, collecting titles at home and abroad. He made an impact as soon as he was old enough to race cars, too, winning the Formula Ford Festival at Brands Hatch in 2000 and also the McLaren Autosport BRDC Young Driver award, landing a test in a McLaren and considerable kudos. Anthony flew in Formula Three, too, ending 2001 as the fastest driver in the British series, but having to settle for being runner-up behind team-mate Takuma Sato. A lack of budget precluded a move to Formula One feeder category Formula 3000, but Anthony made his Formula One debut before the 2002 season was out, standing in for Alex Yoong at Minardi. His pace and feedback earned Anthony a test driver's role with British American Racing then Honda, but it was only when he joined Super Aguri Racing in 2007, as team-mate to Sato, that he became a full-time racer again.

FORCE INDIA F1

Three name changes in four years can confuse, but the team that was once Jordan has an identity that ought to stick, in Force India F1, and it stands to take Formula One to a new audience. There's an injection of cash, but it will take time to bear fruit.

Another new livery and another new owner, but this one might work.

Nothing stands still in Formula One for long, but the pace of change for the team that was not so long ago famously identifiable and loved as Jordan has been extraordinary. Hopefully, now that Indian race fan and billionaire Vijay Mallya – chairman of the world's second largest brewers, United Breweries – has taken the reins, some stability and a clear identity will be regained. Indeed, Mallya has great ambitions to make it the most identified-with team in Asia, the focus for India's gargantuan population and beyond.

Before you think of this team in terms of what it has (not) achieved in its recent incarnations as Midland F1 then Spyker, don't forget that this team is one with four grand prix wins to its credit from when it was Jordan and some of the staff who helped the likes of Damon Hill, Heinz-Harald Frentzen and Giancarlo Fisichella to those wins are still on the payroll.

Look at the raw ingredients for 2008 and changes ought to go way beyond the change of livery from Spyker's Dutch orange to Force India F1's white with dark red. Any team that has Mike Gascoyne in charge of its technical development will make progress up the grid. That Mike's input has been bolstered by the return to the fold of one-time Jordan designer Mark Smith

PAST LEGENDS

Damon Hill was World Champion for Williams in 1996, but his smile was probably never as broad as it was at Spa-Francorchamps in 1998 when he won the Belgian GP in the rain to give the team its maiden win. He led home a Jordan one-two in fact, ahead of team-mate Ralf Schumacher, but that was to be his one and only win for Eddie Jordan's team. Ulsterman Eddie Irvine was the first Brit to race for this Irish team based opposite the circuit gates at Silverstone, making that infamous debut in Japan at the end of 1993 when Ayrton Senna punched him. Two full seasons followed, with a pair of third place finishes being his best results. When Irvine moved on to Ferrari in 1996, his place was taken by the team's third British driver, Martin Brundle. Sadly for Martin, this meant that he was to be reunited with the Peugeot V10s that had proved so unreliable for him with McLaren in 1994 and a huge accident in the opening race in Australia got his campaign off to the wrong sort of flying start and he stayed for just one year. Then the team became Midland F1, then Spyker and now it's Force India F1.

from Red Bull to work as Design Director alongside Technical Director James Key shows a determination to improve.

This year's car will be the first that has had Gascoyne's full impact, as he joined the team too late in 2006 to do much about the 2007 car. That the B-spec of last year's F8-VII was such a step forward when it was given its debut in the Belgian GP and Adrian Sutil propelled it up the field past Toyotas and Hondas to fight with the Red Bulls shows that Gascoyne hasn't lost his touch and that Key and the crew can bring a car on if given the budget. The car is based on last year's B-spec car. By running with a Ferrari customer engine again, the design team has been able to concentrate on finding some more downforce.

Team principal Colin Kolles

spent a lot of time last year fighting against rivals Toro Rosso and Super Aguri using customer chassis. Perhaps this year he will be able to concentrate on internal matters.

The input of Mallya's millions will also help the team forward as not only will it allow the design department a freer hand, but it should enable the team to carry out more of those invaluable testing miles that stop any team from falling away from their rivals.

Sutil quickly established himself as the team's lead driver last year, usurping Christijan Albers and scoring the team's only point for eighth place in Japan. As a result of this, he is firmly in the driving seat this year, with the more experienced Giancarlo Fisichella coming in as his team-mate.

A final thought, for stats fans, is that this team – as Spyker – ranked equal fourth on laps led last year. McLaren and Ferrari were way clear, but the team's inspired tyre gamble at the European GP had debutant Markus Winkelhock take the lead on lap 2 as others pitted for wet-weather tyres and he stayed ahead behind the safety car for six laps, putting them very close to Renault's 10 laps in front, but better than BMW Sauber's four. If ever there was a trick question for a quiz, this is it.

FOR THE RECORD

Country of origin:	England
Team base:	Silverstone, England
Telephone:	(44) 01327 850800
Website:	WWW.FORCEINDIAF1.COM
Active in Formula One:	From 1991 (as Midland F1 in 2006 then Spyker in 2007)
Grands Prix contested:	285
Wins:	4
Pole positions:	2
Fastest laps:	2

2007 DRIVERS & RESULTS

Driver	Nationality	Races	Wins	Pts	Pos
Christijan Albers	Dutch	9	0	-	n/a
Adrian Sutil	German	17	0	1	19th
Markus Winkelhock	German	1	0	0	n/a
Sakon Yamamoto	Japanese	7	0	0	n/a

THE TEAM

Team owner:	Vijay Mallya
Team principal:	Colin Kolles
Chief technical officer:	Mike Gascoyne
Chief operations officer:	Patrick Missling
Technical director:	James Key
Design director:	Mark Smith
Chief designer:	John McQuilliam
Head of aerodynamics:	Simon Phillips
Chief engineer:	Dominic Harlow
Team manager:	Andy Stevenson
Chassis:	Force India F1
Engine:	Ferrari V8
Tyres:	Bridgestone

Damon Hill gave Jordan the first of its four wins, at Spa in 1998.

ADRIAN SUTIL

At the start of last year, people were asking "Adrian who?", yet by mid-campaign there were enough messages coming from those in the know that here was a driver of unusual calibre. The car beneath him might make this hard to prove though.

It would be easy enough for Adrian to have an identity crisis as a trained pianist among racing drivers, as someone who is a German-Uruguayan hybrid and someone who drives for Force India F1 which was Spyker, which was Midland F1, which was Jordan. However, his driving puts everything in perspective.

Few drivers offer credit or compliments to a rival, but one of those praising his abilities last year was his Formula Three team-mate from 2005, one Lewis Hamilton. That certainly made critics look and listen.

Indeed, even though he had crashed out of most of his first few grands prix, often on the opening lap, Adrian was even being mentioned in connection with a move to Williams for 2008. Until Kazuki Nakajima nailed down the second ride that is.

Such is the disparity between teams that it's often only informative to judge a driver against his team-mate. This being the case, the rookie outperformed the much more experienced Christijan Albers

Adrian needs to add some consistency to the speed thast he displayed through 2007.

and then both of his replacements. The clearest evidence came when conditions were difficult. Take practice in Monaco when he lapped fastest of all in the wet.

Another example came at the Belgian GP when he passed seven cars in the first five laps to run 12th, looking at home as he put pressure on David Coulthard's Red Bull.

Adrian will do well to remember though that a driver is often seen as being as good only as his last drive and, racing for Force India F1 might not offer him the machine in which to stand out. the good news from Adrian's stand-point though is that new team owner Vijay Mallya is already a fan.

TRACK NOTES

Nationality:	GERMAN
Born:	11 JANUARY 1983, GRAFELFING, GERMANY
Website:	WWW.ADRIANSUTIL.COM
Teams:	SPYKER/FORCE INDIA F1 2007-2008

CAREER RECORD	
First Grand Prix:	2007 AUSTRALIAN GP
Grand Prix starts:	17
Grand Prix wins:	0
	Best result: eighth, 2007 Japanese GP
Poles:	0
Fastest laps:	0
Points:	1
Honours:	2006 JAPANESE FORMULA THREE CHAMPION, 2005 EUROPEAN FORMULA THREE RUNNER-UP, 2002 SWISS FORMULA FORD CHAMPION

CAREER HISTORY

After showing well in karting but not winning any international titles, Adrian moved up to cars in 2002 and promptly won the Swiss Formula Ford crown. He tried German Formula BMW in 2003 and ranked sixth. His raw speed was displayed when he twice qualified on pole position in his first year of European Formula Three in 2004 when racing for current team boss Adrian Kolles. For 2005, Adrian moved across to the crack ASM team alongside Lewis Hamilton, ending the year as runner-up to his team-mate with a pair of wins at Spa-Francorchamps and the Nurburgring, plus second place in the Marlboro Masters invitation Formula Three race at Zandvoort. While Hamilton moved on to glory in GP2 in 2006, Adrian tried cars with more power by racing Germany's A1GP entry. By the end of 2006, he acted as the Friday driver for Spyker for the final three grands prix and did sufficiently well to land a race seat for 2007.

GIANCARLO FISICHELLA

He's won three grands prix. He's raced for a team that topped the tables – Renault in 2005 and 2006 – but he's missed the biggest prize of all and, having been dropped by Renault, he's now drinking in the last chance saloon with Force India F1.

Finishing fourth overall in 2006, albeit three places behind team-mate Fernando Alonso who became world champion must seem a very long time ago, for the 2007 campaign was a grim one for Giancarlo.

Faced with a rookie team-mate of great potential in Heikki Kovalainen ought to have made a change from being very much number two to Alonso.

However, it didn't work out as well as he'd hoped and the sundry points collected in the first half of the season all but dried up after the British GP in July.

Fourth place in Monaco, a circuit on which he has always shone, was the highlight of a poor season.

Worse than being outscored 21 to 30 by Kovalainen as he ranked eighth overall was the fact that the Finn had assumed the role of being Renault's number one by getting to grips better with a car, the R27, that had some major handling flaw.

With all of the disturbance in the drivers' market at the close of last season that was

Giancarlo brings experience to the party, rejoining a team he last raced for in 2003.

precipitated by Alonso's departure from McLaren, Giancarlo was linked with a move to Williams, but with Nico Rosberg staying on he was suddenly looking at drives with

an assortment of other teams, which was less than dignified for a driver of his standing. Only landing a seat at Force India F1 – a team that was once his old alma mater Jordan – saved his career.

Giancarlo's sideline is a racing team, running cars in Formula One's feeder category, GP2. However, what will possibly fill Giancarlo's retirement years, whenever they commence, is a racing academy that he is planning to set up in Italy to train engineers, mechanics and team managers.

TRACK NOTES

Nationality:	ITALIAN
Born:	14 JANUARY, 1973, ROME, ITALY
Website:	WWW.GIANCARLOFISICHELLA.IT
Teams:	MINARDI 1996, JORDAN 1997 & 2002-2003, BENETTON 1998-2001, SAUBER 2004, RENAULT 2005-2007, FORCE INDIA F1 2008
CAREER RECORD	
First Grand Prix:	1996 AUSTRALIAN GP
Grand Prix starts:	196
Grand Prix wins:	3
	2003 BRAZILIAN GP, 2005 AUSTRALIAN GP, 2006 Malaysian GP
Poles:	3
Fastest laps:	2
Points:	267
Honours:	1994 ITALIAN FORMULA THREE & MONACO FORMULA THREE CHAMPION

CAREER HISTORY

Small and lightweight, it's no surprise Giancarlo fared well in karts. Runner-up at European level in 1989 and then at world level in 1990, he was much sought after when he graduated to Formula Three in 1992. The highlight of this three-year sojourn was winning the Monaco support race in 1994 as well as the Italian title that year. With no budget to graduate to Formula 3000, he was signed by Alfa Romeo to race in the International Touring Car Championship, in which he impressed. Minardi signed him for 1996, but his Formula One debut year was cut short when a driver with money, Giovanni Lavaggi, replaced him mid-season. Jordan wanted Giancarlo for 1997 and he starred. By 1998, he was racing for Benetton, but it was only when he returned to Jordan in 2002 that he became a winner, at Interlagos in 2003. A year with Sauber yielded nothing, but he joined Renault in 2005 and won in Australia, adding another in Malaysia in 2006.

McLAREN

Last year could have been the ultimate return to what this illustrious team considers its natural niche: at the top. There was a double world champion and a super-fast rookie, but also civil war and a spying scandal. This year can only be better.

After its furious 2007 campaign, McLaren wants to drop the drama.

Politicians have a habit of saying that they want to "draw a line" under any failure. So, coming out of a season of magnificent on-track action that was marred by the politics, intrigue and in-fighting in the pit lane and paddock, it's safe to say that McLaren supremo Ron Dennis will also be looking to draw a line under 2007 and start all over again. Indeed, by the Hungarian GP in August, Dennis can surely have never felt so put-upon, not even in the days when his drivers Alain Prost and Ayrton Senna were fighting like cat and dog. Matters seemed to get a stage worse at every turn.

The double tragedy in this is that this was the first season for several years that McLaren was a true frontrunner, able to take on arch-rivals Ferrari.

Making matters even better than it had been in the Mika Hakkinen versus Michael Schumacher battles of 1998 and 1999, both drivers from each team were capable of winning as Fernando Alonso and Lewis Hamilton took on Kimi Raikkonen and Felipe Massa. Sadly for Dennis and his dreams of glory, Alonso and Hamilton also took on each other, something that excited onlookers, and Dennis too in many ways, as he loves to give both drivers an equal chance and cock a snook at the way that Ferrari inevitably favours one driver over another,

PAST LEGENDS

Founded by a Kiwi, but based in Britain, McLaren has run a host of British drivers during its illustrious history, but mainly in cameo roles. Of the regulars, those given a lengthy run-out, David Coulthard enjoyed the longest stint, taking 12 of his 13 wins with the team, and finishing as runner-up in 2001. James Hunt went a step better and became World Champion for McLaren in 1976. While John Watson came within five points of a similar accolade in 1982. Nigel Mansell never quite fitted in at McLaren, literally, in 1995, while Martin Brundle's hopes of glory were scuppered in 1994 by the team using Peugeot power. It was little better the following year for Mark Blundell when Mercedes joined up. Former motorcycle champion Mike Hailwood hoped for great things when he was fielded in a third car in 1974, but a broken leg ended that. Peter Gethin, Brian Redman, Vic Elford, John Surtees, David Hobbs, Jackie Oliver and Derek Bell all also had a go, but it's safe to say that the driver who set McLaren's gold standard was Ayrton Senna, with his 35 wins and three world titles.

most famously in the years that Schumacher led the team. However, this and this alone cost both his drivers the chance to be crowned champion.

Well, that and the spying scandal, something that was still rumbling on at the end of last year. Lest you've forgotten, that centred on a disgruntled Ferrari employee allegedly sending 780 pages of classified Ferrari documentation to McLaren's chief designer Mike Coughlan last spring. The outcome was that McLaren had all of its points towards the constructors' championship deleted and was fined a massive $100m.

Before moving on from McLaren's 2007 campaign, it's worth pointing out that the atmosphere at the team became so poisonous that Alonso elected to leave with two years still running on his contract.

The shame of this all, of something that promised so much and only just failed to deliver the ultimate prize, was that it all got so nasty. Indeed, the bickering masked the fact that the MP4-22 was the best McLaren for years and something of which the design team could be justly proud as it showed that not only Adrian Newey could produce race-winning cars for McLaren, with a tally of eight wins from 17 grands prix plus eight poles and five fastest laps endorsing its attributes.

The engineers did their bit too, as there was not one mechanical failure. That the most public failure suffered all year was a strategic one was embarrassing and you can be sure that the parties involved in keeping Hamilton out for just another lap or two until the rain was likely to stop in China will haunt them to this day.

So, what has changed for this year? Not a lot, really, which has to be good in terms of looking forwards to another competitive car. Obviously, there is a new driver in Heikki Kovalainen coming in alongside Hamilton, in a straight swap with Alonso. But, whatever happens at McLaren, not one employee at Woking or at Mercedes High Performance Engines in Brixworth can be under any illusion that Hamilton and his legions of fans expect a world title this year.

FOR THE RECORD

Country of origin:	England
Team base:	Woking, England
Telephone:	(44) 01483 728211
Website:	WWW.McLAREN.COM
Active in Formula One:	From 1966
Grands Prix contested:	631
Wins:	156
Pole positions:	133
Fastest laps:	134

2007 DRIVERS & RESULTS

Driver	Nationality	Races	Wins	Pts	Pos
Fernando Alonso	Spanish	17	4	109	3rd
Lewis Hamilton	British	17	4	109	2nd

THE TEAM

Team principal:	Ron Dennis
Chief operating officer:	Martin Whitmarsh
Engineering director:	Paddy Lowe
Design & Development Director:	Neal Oatley
Head of aerodynamics:	Simon Lacey
Chief engineer:	Tim Goss
Head of race operations:	Steve Hallam
Team manager:	Dave Ryan
Test driver:	tba
Chassis:	MP4-23
Engine:	Mercedes V8
Tyres:	Bridgestone

James Hunt joined McLaren in 1976 and beat Niki Lauda to the title.

LEWIS HAMILTON

It's hard to know where to start when considering what has gone before and what lies ahead of this remarkable British driver. What's safe to say is that no-one has ever made such an impact as a rookie and, amazingly, only the world title will do in 2008.

The domination of Formula One by Michael Schumacher almost killed Formula One because the German great's rampant success had made the sport predictable.

That FIA president Max Mosley saw fit to comment that Lewis could do similar damage on the evidence of just one racing season and before he has even been crowned shows how high the expectations surrounding him have become.

Yes, he could have been champion last year. Indeed, should have been, as he had been 12 points clear with just two rounds to run. But he wasn't, falling one run short. Formula One supremo Bernie Ecclestone has even suggested that it was a good thing that he lost out to Kimi Raikkonen at the final round, as it would give Lewis something to aim for as he heads into his second year of Formula One.

Looking back, the fact that Lewis cheekily passed his double world champion team-mate Fernando Alonso at the first corner of the opening grand prix probably started what would become the rot at

Lewis knows that he will be under the spotlight after his staggering rookie year.

McLaren. The result was a team at war with itself. Then the wins started flowing as a result not only of his pure speed but also the phenomenal level of preparedness that he had coached into him by McLaren

and he had to learn to deal with soaring media expectation. Then there was the spying scandal and finally incidents under pressure in Japan, China and Brazil, so there's scope for improvement, which must scare his rivals rigid.

TRACK NOTES

Nationality:	BRITISH
Born:	7 JANUARY 1985, STEVENAGE, ENGLAND
Website:	WWW.LEWISHAMILTON.COM
Teams:	McLAREN 2007-2008

CAREER RECORD

First Grand Prix:	2007 AUSTRALIAN GP
Grand Prix starts:	17
Wins:	4
	2007 Canadian GP, United States GP, Hungarian GP, Japanese GP
Pole positions:	6
Fastest laps:	2
Points:	109
Honours:	2007 FORMULA ONE RUNNER-UP, 2006 GP2 CHAMPION, 2005 EUROPEAN FORMULA THREE CHAMPION, 2003 BRITISH FORMULA RENAULT CHAMPION, 2000 WORLD KART CUP CHAMPION & EUROPEAN FORMULA A KARTING CHAMPION, 1999 ITALIAN INTERCONTINENTAL A KARTING CHAMPION, 1996 McLAREN MERCEDES CHAMPION OF THE FUTURE, 1995 BRITISH CADET KARTING CHAMPION

CAREER HISTORY

It's almost easier to list what Lewis didn't win in his garlanded journey from cadet karter to Formula One. Yet, as he gathered title after title, the biggest success he had was to attract the patronage of McLaren's Ron Dennis. Not only did this enable Lewis to enjoy the best equipment, but also all the advice that McLaren could offer in making Lewis professional in every sense of the word. Lewis spent 2002 learning Formula Renault and then became British champion in 2003. His European Formula Three quest also took two years to yield the title, with notable wins on the streets of Monaco and Macau. But, if anyone doubted Lewis's ability, the way with which he blitzed GP2 - Formula One's feeder formula - in 2006 vanquished any concerns, with a couple of drives through the field after problems leaving jaws hanging.

HEIKKI KOVALAINEN

From being castigated after his maiden grand prix, Heikki became Renault's team leader. But Alonso's return meant that he had to leave and yet this might work to his advantage as he will be racing an infinitely more competitive McLaren.

Small, upbeat and effervescent, Heikki gives the appearance of being an irrepressible force. Trouble is, this didn't appear to be the case in the first half of 2007 despite covering more miles as Renault's test driver in 2006 than anyone else. It was almost as though Heikki had been found out, his skill level just short of the top drawer. However, look harder and it was clear that his Renault team-mate Giancarlo Fisichella was also not setting the world on fire for the team that had been champions in 2006. In short, the Renault R27 wasn't a gem and it certainly wasn't the car with which to try and make your name in Formula One. It was unpredictable and not conducive to encouraging all-out attack.

By year's end, with a best finish of second in the rain and poor visibility of the Fuji Speedway after resisting all that evential world champion Kimi Raikkonen could throw at him, Heikki ranked seventh. Most importantly, he'd scored more points than Fisichella, a Formula One veteran of 12 years. In that, he earned major respect.

After a straight swap with Alonso, Heikki will be looking for equality with Lewis. And wins.

At this point, when he was being linked with a move to McLaren in a direct swap with the disenchanted Fernando Alonso, he owned up that he had perhaps not put enough thought into what it takes, both physically and mentally, to become world champion. And, in that, he did something unusual for a Formula One driver: he admitted that he was less than perfect, making him all the more likely to succeed.

Heikki ought to be around Formula One for years and his buoyant character as much as his speed will make him a popular member of any team, the sort for whom the whole team will work flat-out.

TRACK NOTES

Nationality:	FINNISH
Born: 19 OCTOBER 1981, SUOMUSSALMI, FINLAND	
Website:	WWW.HEIKKIKOVALAINEN.NET
Teams:	RENAULT 2007
	MCLAREN 2008

CAREER RECORD	
First Grand Prix:	2007 AUSTRALIAN GP
Grand Prix starts:	17
Wins:	0
	best result: second, 2007 Japanese GP
Pole positions:	0
Fastest laps:	0
Points:	30
Honours:	2005 GP2 RUNNER-UP,
	2004 FORMULA NISSAN WORLD SERIES
	CHAMPION, 2004 CHAMPION OF CHAMPIONS
	AT RACE OF CHAMPIONS,
	2000 NORDIC KARTING CHAMPION

CAREER HISTORY

Contemporary kart racers in Scandinavia knew of Heikki's abilities in the 1990s, but these were put onto a larger stage in 2001 when he raced in British Formula Renault and took a couple of wins. Fortec Motorsport ran him in British Formula Three in 2002. Again, he picked up speed as the year progressed and bagged two wins to rank third overall before finishing second in the invitation street race in Macau. The more powerful World Series by Nissan followed, and his one win in 2003 was followed by six more and the title in 2004. But what really put Heikki's name up in lights was his victory in the multi-discipline Race of Champions that winter, beating one Michael Schumacher. Renault signed him as a test driver for 2005, alongside his GP2 campaign in which Nico Rosberg pipped him. Then 2006 was spent testing for Renault before landing his full-time ride for 2007.

TALKING POINT:
TRANSPORTERS

Long gone are the days when even Ferrari's cars were transported to the circuits on the roof of an open-topped truck. Today's Formula One transporters are tailor-made, multi-purpose and extremely expensive.

A top Formula One team will bring a minimum of three 40-ton transporters to a grand prix. One carries the two race cars, the spare and a fourth monocoque from which a spare spare can be built up if need be. The second transporter carries the engines and computer equipment, with the third taking the workshop equipment, refuelling rigs and spare parts. With Bridgestone supplying tyres to all the teams, at least this is one element, and a bulky one, that the teams no longer need to take with them.

The teams used to take a couple of motorhomes to each race from which to feed the staff and VIP guests, but these have been outmoded with enormous multi-storey temporary buildings being erected in their place in the paddock.

The transporters are sleek and corporate on the outside and tailor-made on the inside.

Inside the transporters, everything is fitted not only to maximise space but also to ease the finding of the thousands of tools and parts that must be taken to each event.

These beasts of burden also extend hydraulically either upwards or outwards and sometimes in both directions to open out into team offices, with rooms for those crucial driver debriefs after every session on the track.

As the largest flat objects the teams take to the races, the transporters act as billboards not only on the road but when they reach their destination, so all are decked out in team livery and the photographers love them.

It's safe to say that the transporters don't come cheap, costing over £1m apiece.

The transporters are driven to the circuits from the teams' respective bases in England, Germany, Italy and Switzerland, usually arriving on the Wednesday before the race, with FIA officials checking that they are lined up with inch-perfect precision behind their respective pit garages, with their tractor units facing the lines of team hospitality palaces.

Then, with Formula One being as it is, with presentation being of paramount importance, every transporter is hosed down and polished, ready for the arrival of the rest of the team on the Thursday.

Traditionally, the transporters will cover as many as 38,000km for the European-

Corporate image is important, but the transporters must first and foremost perform their intended role.

based grands prix, with the test team transporter all but echoing this figure on its separate route around the continent.

For the races outside Europe, known as 'flyaways', the transporters are left at base after the cars and specially-made freight cases have been delivered to an airport, loaded onto special pallets and then flown together under the auspices of FOM (Formula One Management), with each team allowed 10 tons of payload and having to pay extra for anything above that. A typical bill is £300,000 per race.

TALKING POINT:
ROBERT KUBICA'S AMAZING ESCAPE

Every now and again Formula One is rocked by an accident of mammoth proportions. Such is the strength of the cockpit these days that the drivers clamber out, often without assistance, but you're left wondering how.

To see a Formula One car crash at high speed is frightening enough, as you can never be sure where and when they will stop. But to see one literally explode takes your breath away.

Robert Kubica had one such accident in the Canadian Grand Prix last year and even seasoned observers gasped as they thought they were witnessing a fatality. Thanks to the sheer strength of the monocoque of his BMW Sauber, Robert not only survived the 75g impact with the barriers but suffered little more than minor concussion and a sprained ankle, something that was all the more amazing as the front end of the tub was ripped open and the F1.07 came to a halt with the Pole's feet visible.

You could say that it was a miracle, which in some ways it was, especially as the car flew back across the traffic, but Robert's survival was testament to the stringent safety specifications that the insisted upon.

The accident happened on the 27th lap of the 70-lap race when Robert had lost position after a scrambled pit stop during a safety car period. He was pushing to make up ground and was anxious to pass Jarno Trulli's Toyota which had got ahead of him on their out lap. Arriving at the left kink before the hairpin at around 175mph, Robert was caught out by his closing speed and clipped the left rear wheel of the Toyota

and, with his car's nose jammed under the Toyota's rear wheels, flipped up and vaulted over the grass verge directly into one of the surrounding concrete walls, hitting it at an oblique angle at 145mph.

The wall was angled towards the track rather than running parallel, as it protected an opening for course vehicles to come onto the track if needed, and the BMW Sauber's next impact was with the wall beyond the opening, ripping off three wheels after which a violent series followed as he bounced back towards the track.

The F1.07 then dug into the grass verge and this flipped it as it crossed back onto the track, doing a half roll before it hit the crash barriers on the other side of the circuit. As this was happening, one of Robert's wheels struck him on the helmet.

Robert's plans to 'return to the saddle' for the following weekend's US Grand Prix were thwarted at Indianapolis when he failed a mental dexterity test and doctors voiced concerns that a further impact would harm him, but he was back for the French GP.

RIGHT: Having hit Jarno Trulli's Toyota, Robert Kubica's BMW Sauber flies over the grass verge, slams into a retaining wall before firing back across the track. Luckily, the survival cell did its job.

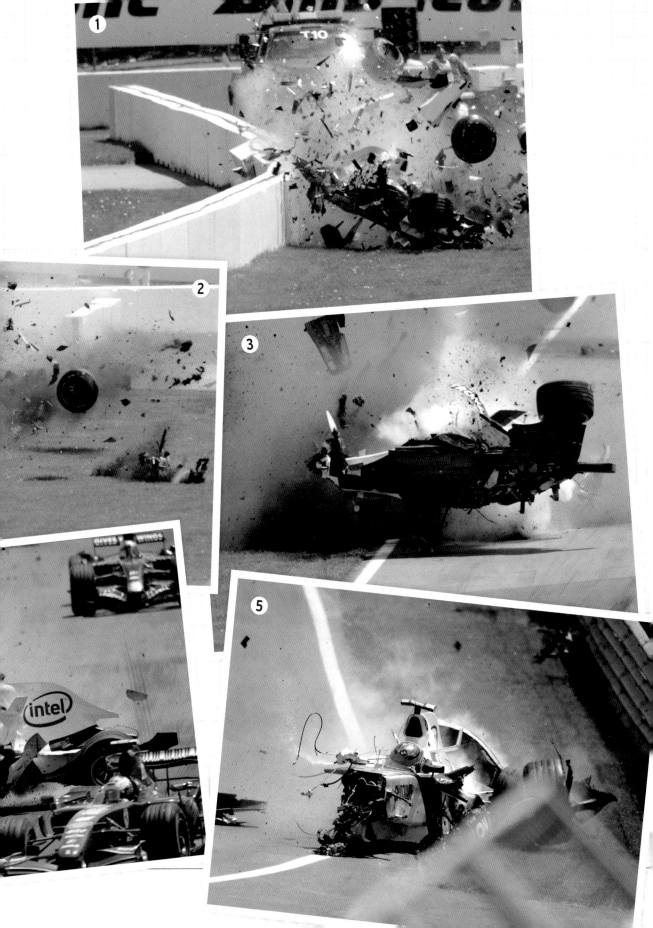

KNOW THE TRACKS 2008

Changes come most years to the Formula One calendar, but 2008 has moved the rate of change up several gears with the introduction not only of two new circuits in Valencia and Singapore, but they're street circuits to boot. To be even more different, the Singapore GP will be run after dark to create an image like none before it. Times they are a-changing. American fans on the other hand will have to watch solely on TV, as their race at Indianapolis has been canned.

Since the demise of the Phoenix circuit in the scrubby deserts of Arizona in 1991, Monaco has stood alone as the only street circuit on the Formula One bill of fare. Certainly, it's the most famous street circuit by far, with its form feeding way past its famous casino and along the fabled harbour front. Valencia and Singapore have been designed with a similar sentiment, but their execution is very different and their backdrops not likely to be confused.

It could be said that Adelaide, used until 1995, was a street circuit, but that was more one in a parkland setting in a downtown area. Likewise, the circuit that succeeded it as the home of the Australian GP – Melbourne's Albert Park – is also downtown, but it at least has a flow of its own that's not dictated by any right-angled street corners.

The element of having a night race will be novel indeed, the thinking behind this is that this will ensure that the grand prix is held when European fans have risen from their beds, thus boosting

the television audience. If it works, Sepang and Melbourne may well follow suit and run their races after dark.

The Australian GP sets the ball rolling again in mid-March, with the Malaysian GP at Sepang following. The dust and rocks of Bahrain provide a third very different setting for the third round before Formula One reaches it spiritual home of Europe for the first of two races in Fernando Alonso's home country, this one at Barcelona's Circuit de Catalunya.

One of the biggest changes is the movement of the Turkish GP from its established late-August slot to one in mid-May, which at least means that the hills behind the popular and challenging circuit will look green rather than sun-bleached brown. Then comes Monaco, the annual chance to see and be seen, and for the drivers to practice the art of trying to thread their cars through the eye of a needle.

The North American jaunt has just the one race in 2008, with the Canadian GP remaining and the United States GP up on blocks. It may return to the Indianapolis Motor Speedway, but it could also be given to Las Vegas for 2009.

After Canada comes that long-standing sequence of French, British, German and Hungarian GPs, with Silverstone set for another bumper crowd as the Lewis Hamilton phenomenon continues to spread and grow, but then comes something new. This is the European GP and that doesn't mean a grand prix at the Nurburgring. Instead, it's on the track built around the harbour front in Valencia, over the quays of the port that was home to the America's Cup yachting extravaganza.

This takes us through to the start of September when the drivers will have their annual fix of Spa-Francorchamps and the challenges and thrills that it offers before heading to Monza for the high-speed flow that this oldest of old circuits still offers.

The wrap-up to the 18-race campaign starts with the Singapore night race before Fuji Speedway (hopefully without the rain this year), Shanghai (ditto) and Brazil's Interlagos circuits concludes the voting on the first weekend of November.

Despite all of this change to the Formula One World Championship calendar, there are still more nations that want to follow the lead of Valencia and Singapore in getting into the circus for the kudos and excitement that it brings. Russia continues to tilt for a grand prix and so does India. Beating both to it, and introducing another new street circuit believe it or not, is Abu Dhabi, which has its race deal for 2009 already signed, sealed and delivered.

So, one thing that is for sure is that Formula One is back on the road again, with the explosion of popularity that Lewis Hamilton triggered in his astounding rookie season in 2007 being felt all around the globe.

MELBOURNE

Win here and the season will probably be kind to you, but the venue for the first race of the season can often throw up a surprise result before teams find their true form.

Change is afoot. Tradition was restored with Australia regaining its position as hosting the opening race, but there has been talk that the race might be held under lights, after dark, so that it will be run when the European audience is awake, rather than in the small hours of the morning when not so many fans have risen from their beds. The 2008 opener will be held in Australian daylight hours, but Formula One supremo Bernie Ecclestone made it plain last year that he expects the Australian GP to run as a night race in the future.

The Albert Park circuit is a good place to start a season as the weather is almost always bright and the crowd overflowing the grandstands. With Melbourne's cityscape in the background, it's a most attractive venue.

The track itself offers a combination of corners, leaving it neither tight and twisty nor fast and flowing, but somewhere in between, offering some scope for all sorts of cars.

There's almost always someone left in the gravel trap at Turn 1 on lap 1 and usually a bit of wheel-banging on the narrow entry to Turn 3. After that, though, the track opens out, particularly once it comes out from under the trees at Turn 6, Marina. Clark Chicane interrupts the flow on the far side of the lake, but the sweeper that follows is excellent, with drivers pitching up at the Waite esses around a blind entry. At Ascari, a tight right, a few brave souls try to pass, but it's tricky. A good exit out of Prost is required to have a chance of overtaking into Turn 1.

The day it all began: Races were held in Albert Park in the 1950s, but the modern iteration was made in this downtown park for 1997, when Damon Hill won for Williams in a race that would have gone to team-mate Jacques Villeneuve on his debut but for failing oil pressure late on.

Do you remember when?: One of the most celebrated Australian GPs at Albert Park was held in 1998. Sadly, it's remembered for the wrong reasons, for David Coulthard voluntarily ceding the lead to his McLaren team-mate Mika Hakkinen to honour a pre-race agreement that whichever of them led into the first corner would go on to win the race. This was Hakkinen, but he misheard a radio message and called in for a pit stop that hadn't been called and the delay of this drive through, put him behind Coulthard and had to be rectified.

Best for action: A lack of grip is the chief concern, which is typical of temporary street circuits. It's hard on brakes too.

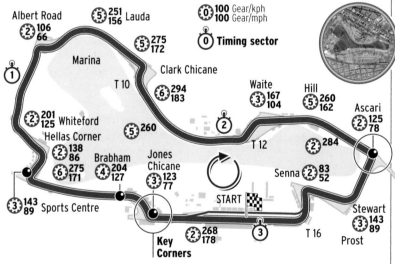

Albert Road
(5) 251/156 Lauda
(2) 106/66

(5) 275/172

(0) 100 Gear/kph / 100 Gear/mph

(0) Timing sector

Marina

T 10

Clark Chicane

(6) 294/183

Waite (3) 167/104

Hill (5) 260/162

Ascari (2) 125/78

(2) 201/125 Whiteford

Hellas Corner
(2) 138/86

(5) 260

(2) 284

(1)

Brabham (4) 204/127

(6) 275/171

Jones Chicane (3) 123/77

T 12

Senna (2) 83/52

(3) 143/89 Sports Centre

START

(3)

Stewart (3) 143/89

Key Corners

(2) 268/178

(3)

T 16

Prost

2007 POLE TIME: Raikkonen (Ferrari), 1m26.072s, 137.815mph/221.792kph

2007 FASTEST LAP: Raikkonen (Ferrari), 1m25.235s, 139.173mph/223.978kph

2007 WINNER'S AVERAGE SPEED: 134.156mph/215.904kph

LAP RECORD: M Schumacher (Ferrari), 1m24.125s, 141.016mph/226.933kph, 2004

SEPANG

The Sepang circuit offers great scope for passing, but watch carefully this year, as it might be the last time you see it in daylight, as night races beckon.

Long seen as the jewel in South-East Asia's crown, Malaysia's purpose-built Sepang circuit found itself under new pressure in 2007 when plans were announced for neighbouring Singapore to hold a grand prix from this spring. Formula One supremo Bernie Ecclestone had long wanted a race there and as Sepang's contract had only until 2010 to run, it was time to start talking. You could tell that the pressure was on, especially when Ecclestone started referring to its eight-year-old facilities looking "shabby". They are not particularly, but perhaps this is how he convinced the race organisers that they might need to hold future grands prix after nightfall.

Tests were carried out at Paul Ricard in September, with portable floodlights, and Renault test driver Nelson Piquet Jr said everything felt normal.

The Sepang circuit is great for racing and has a fabulous flow. The first corner always provides excitement on lap 1 as it doubles back on itself and then Turn 2 does the same, so the right line out of Turn 1 isn't necessarily the right one into Turn 2. The unusual width of the track is key to overtaking, and the run from Turn 3 to Turn 8 can provide side-by-side racing as long as all parties are sensible.

The prime overtaking spots, though, are up the straight behind the main grandstand and into the final corner, then again into Turn 1 at the start of the following lap.

INSIDE TRACK

MALAYSIAN GRAND PRIX

Date:	**23 March**
Circuit name:	**Sepang**
Circuit length:	**3.444 miles/5.542km**
Number of laps:	**56**
Telephone:	**00 60 3 85262000**
Website:	**www.malaysiangp.com.my**

PREVIOUS WINNERS	
1999	**Eddie Irvine** FERRARI
2000	**Michael Schumacher** FERRARI
2001	**Michael Schumacher** FERRARI
2002	**Ralf Schumacher** WILLIAMS
2003	**Kimi Raikkonen** McLAREN
2004	**Michael Schumacher** FERRARI
2005	**Fernando Alonso** RENAULT
2006	**Giancarlo Fisichella** RENAULT
2007	**Fernando Alonso** McLAREN

The day it all began: It seemed like a brave new world in 1999 when Sepang was the first of the new wave of super tracks from the pen of Hermann Tilke. Mika Hakkinen arrived with a two-point advantage over Ferrari's Eddie Irvine. Michael Schumacher, returning from breaking his leg, rode shotgun and helped Irvine win. Then their cars were disqualified for having oversized bargeboards, but were later reinstated. It was a messy start.

Do you remember when?: In 2001, heavy rain hit on the second lap. The Ferraris of Schumacher and Rubens Barrichello were first and second and both slid off, leaving Jarno Trulli in the lead for Jordan as the safety car came out. Despite falling to 11th, Michael came back to win from Rubens after Ferrari played a masterstroke by putting their drivers onto intermediates.

What makes it difficult?: The searing temperatures combined with soaring humidity. Also, if the rain comes, it really comes. Snakes in the grass can make a retirement seem even worse.

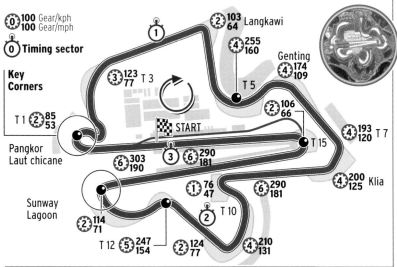

2007 POLE TIME: **Massa (Ferrari),**
1m35.043s, 130.450mph/209.940kph
2007 FASTEST LAP: **Hamilton (McLaren),**
1m36.701s, 128.224mph/206.357kph

2007 WINNER'S AVERAGE SPEED:
125.451mph/201.894kph
LAP RECORD: **Montoya (Williams),**
1m34.223s, 131.595mph/211.772kph, 2004

BAHRAIN

This grand prix stands out for being different, for being in the Middle East and for being in a desert. Spectators are few, but the teams love the facilities.

The Malaysian GP, the race before this one, cooks the drivers with its heat and humidity. So, despite the mercury rising towards the top of the thermometer again, drivers find their visit to this Arab state a relief as it's as arid as it can be and thus far less sapping.

One of the reasons that the circuit was built where it is is down to the fact that it's one of the few places in Bahrain that offers any gradient. In a quest to make some features on an otherwise bland landscape, the designers elected to split the circuit into two zones, the 'oasis' zone around the pits in which the track is surrounded by heavily-watered grass verges and towering grandstands and then the desert zone.

As far as racing is concerned, the circuit at Sakhir offers many more overtaking possibilities than the norm, with four straights leading into tight corners, which is always the desired format for passing.

The circuit also provides one of the most exacting and exciting sequence of bends from Turn 5 to Turn 7, with a wonderfully fast left-right-left sequence that is every bit as exciting as Becketts at Silverstone. If it's not tricky enough in its own right, the added element of a dust coating should a driver run off the racing line makes life interesting for driver and spectator alike.

The final corner is also always worth watching, with many happy to run out over the kerbs when in the heat of battle.

INSIDE TRACK

BAHRAIN GRAND PRIX

Date:	**6 April**
Circuit name:	**Bahrain International Circuit**
Circuit length:	**3.366 miles/5.417km**
Number of laps:	**57**
Telephone:	**00 973 406222**
Website:	**www.bahraingp.com.bh**

PREVIOUS WINNERS

2004	**Michael Schumacher** FERRARI
2005	**Fernando Alonso** RENAULT
2006	**Fernando Alonso** RENAULT
2007	**Felipe Massa** FERRARI

The day it all began: Like Sepang and Shanghai, this tailor-made circuit came from the offices of circuit architect Hermann Tilke and its maiden appearance in 2004 provided a backdrop like no other, with dust a problem. Not that this slowed Michael Schumacher and his Ferrari steamroller. Such was his dominance that year that this was the third race, so it marked his third win as he led throughout, with only team-mate Rubens Barrichello for company. The best of the rest, BAR's Jenson Button, was close on 30s down.

Do you remember when?: Bahrain hosted the season-opener in 2006 and there was a mighty scrap for the lead between Renault's Fernando Alonso and Michael Schumacher. The Ferrari ace had started on pole, but the Spaniard had qualified with more fuel and emerged from his first stop ahead, leaving him to hold off the rampant German for the rest of the race.

What makes it difficult?: Heavy use of the brakes is a feature - into Turns 1, 3, 5 and 7 in particular - which is less than ideal as the ambient temperature is far higher than F1's norm to start with. Engine cooling must be watched out for, too. And, despite glue being sprayed onto the track surround to limit sand storms every time the wind blows, dust blowing onto the track remains an Achilles' heel.

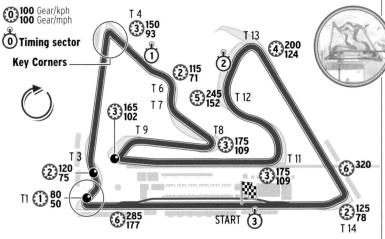

100 Gear/kph
100 Gear/mph
Timing sector
Key Corners

T 4 — 150 93
T 13 — 200 124
115 71
245 152 — T 12
T 6
T 7
165 102
T 9
T 8 — 175 109
T 3
T 11 — 175 109
120 75
320
T1 — 80 50
125 78 — T 14
285 177
START
2007 POLE TIME: Massa (Ferrari), 1m32.652s, 130.786mph/210.480kph

2007 FASTEST LAP: Massa (Ferrari), 1m34.067s, 128.720mph/207.155kph

2007 WINNER'S AVERAGE SPEED: 122.987mph/197.929kph

LAP RECORD: M Schumacher (Ferrari), 1m30.252s, 134.260mph/216.061kph, 2004

BARCELONA

Reshaped for 2007, the Circuit de Catalunya will be filled to capacity as long as Fernando Alonso continues racing, making a wonderful sea of partisan support.

The owners of the Circuit de Catalunya are faced with a new challenge in 2008, a second grand prix in Spain. This is the European GP, to be held in Valencia and it's the direct result of the considerable boom in popularity of Formula One in Spain due to Fernando Alonso's phenomenal success. However, their race is safe, as a contract has been signed that takes it through to 2016.

Due to a considerable amount of testing here, the drivers know this track better than any other. Perhaps that is why they were so upset when the final corner was reshaped ahead of last year's race. Instead of a right-hander that was imperative to get right in order to carry as much speed as possible into the longest straight used in Formula One,

there was a new left-right chicane. Although the new corner broke the flow, there was every chance that it would encourage overtaking, and mercifully it did.

The first part of the circuit is unchanged, with main straight dropping into Turn 1, Elf. the short run to Turn 2 makes this an esse and someone inevitably takes to the gravel trap on lap 1. The track climbs through Renault and Repsol to Lauda before plunging down to Wurth, then rising like a switchback to Campsa. This is on the crest of a hill and a good exit is a must for drivers as it feeds onto the only other straight of note. La Caixa has been tightened in recent years, with the climb to Banc Sabadell and fall to the new chicane completing the lap.

INSIDE TRACK

SPANISH GRAND PRIX

Date:	**27 April**
Circuit name:	**Circuit de Catalunya**
Circuit length:	**2.875 miles/4.627km**
Number of laps:	**65**
Telephone:	**00 34 93 5719771**
Website:	**www.circuitcat.com**

PREVIOUS WINNERS	
1998	**Mika Hakkinen** McLAREN
1999	**Mika Hakkinen** McLAREN
2000	**Mika Hakkinen** McLAREN
2001	**Michael Schumacher** FERRARI
2002	**Michael Schumacher** FERRARI
2003	**Michael Schumacher** FERRARI
2004	**Michael Schumacher** FERRARI
2005	**Kimi Raikkonen** McLAREN
2006	**Fernando Alonso** RENAULT
2007	**Felipe Massa** FERRARI

The day it all began: Jarama outside Madrid hosted the Spanish GP in the 1970s, but Barcelona has always been the spiritual home of the country's big race, with grands prix at Pedralbes, Montjuich Park and then here, with the Circuit de Catalunya making its bow in 1991 when Nigel Mansell triumphed for Williams after an infamous wheel-to-wheel joust down the main straight with McLaren's Ayrton Senna.

Do you remember when?: The rain fell in 1996 and Michael Schumacher scored the first of his 72 wins with Ferrari, sparking hopes of a much-needed revival for the languishing Italian team. That is historic enough, but his win deserves to be celebrated on its own merits as one of the most stunning wet-weather drives of all time, in which he was first home by 45s.

What makes it difficult?: That long, long start/finish straight requires a car that has little drag in a straight line, but the sheer frequency of mid-speed corners has engineers wanting to crank up the wings. So, chassis set-up is always a compromise at the Circuit de Catalunya.

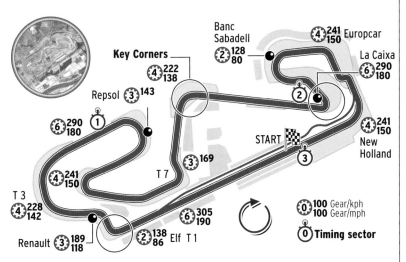

Banc Sabadell — **4** 241/150 Europcar — **2** 128/80 — **Key Corners** — **4** 222/138 — Repsol **3** 143 — La Caixa **6** 290/180 — **6** 290/180 — **1** — **2** — START — **3** — **4** 241/150 New Holland — **3** 169 — T 7 — **4** 241/150 — T 3 — **4** 228/142 — **6** 305/190 — **0** 100/100 Gear/kph Gear/mph — **0** Timing sector — Renault **3** 189/118 — **2** 138/86 Elf T 1

2007 POLE TIME: **Massa (Ferrari)**, 1m21.421s, 124.597mph/200.520kph
2007 FASTEST LAP: **Massa (Ferrari)**, 1m22.680s, 122.700mph/197.467kph

2007 WINNER'S AVERAGE SPEED: 123.044mph/198.021kph
LAP RECORD: **Massa (Ferrari)**, 1m22.680s, 122.700mph/197.467kph, 2007

ISTANBUL

It's not only Felipe Massa, winner here in 2006 and 2007, who likes this modern circuit. All of the drivers do, as it offers them a stern and worthy challenge.

What makes the Istanbul Park Circuit so attractive to the drivers? You could point to a couple of corners, such as the dipping Turn 1, the triple-apex Turn 8 or tight Turn 12 at the end of the back straight. However, they are only components of a package that is by far the finest to have come from the pen of circuit designer Hermann Tilke. When knitted together with the the the other 11 corners of the 3.293-mile lap, there is a certain magic, a sinuous flow and a degree of difficulty that demands excellence.

The first thing that most visitors to this four-year-old circuit notice is the fact that it flows in an anti-clockwise direction. This puts it into an exclusive club of just three with Interlagos and the new Singapore circuit. Weirdly, the first corner is also very reminiscent of the first one at Interlagos, as it drops down an incline as it arcs left. It makes for fireworks on the opening lap and is a potential passing spot thereafter.

Although sunshine is all but guaranteed for this race's regular August spot, there is greater likelihood of mixed weather in 2008 as it has been brought forward to bye the fifth race of the year in mid-May.

In fact, the darkest of clouds lifted last April when the FIA halved the $5m fine hanging over the circuit for its 2006 podium protocol infringement. Indeed, the original fine would probably have bankrupted the Turkish motorsport federation, so the drivers should be truly thankful.

The day it all began: Kimi Raikkonen arrived for the first Turkish GP in 2005 fresh from Formula One's summer break before which he had won in Hungary. He showed his mettle and qualified his McLaren on pole and led every lap of the race in his quest to claw back Fernando Alonso's points advantage, but team-mate Juan Pablo Montoya let him down when he ran wide at Turn 8 with two laps to go and let Alonso through to second.

Do you remember when?: Felipe Massa celebrated his maiden grand prix win at Istanbul in 2006. A pair of second places in the USA and Germany suggested a win might be coming. Pole position helped the Brazilian, as did getting around the tricky first corner first, as his Ferrari team-mate Michael Schumacher locked up behind him when trying to hold off Fernando Alonso's Renault and nearly took him out...

What makes it difficult?: Like Interlagos and now Singapore, the track runs in an anti-clockwise direction. For the engineers, aerodynamic efficiency is a must, but the problem here is that downforce is also needed, especially for the twisting Turn 12-13-14 combination, so no compromise set-up is required. This compromise must also help keep the car on the track at the long and tricky Turn 8.

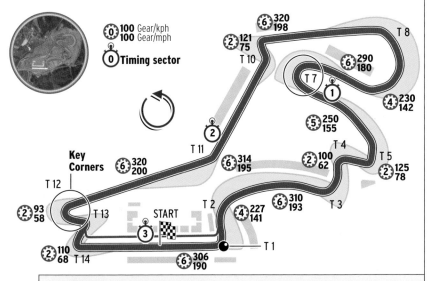

2007 POLE TIME: Massa (Ferrari), 1m27.329s, 136.738mph/220.059kph

2007 FASTEST LAP: Raikkonen (Ferrari), 1m27.295s, 136.786mph/220.136kph

2007 WINNER'S AVERAGE SPEED: 133.040mph/214.108kph

LAP RECORD: Montoya (McLaren), 1m24.770s, 138.096mph/222.167kph, 2005

MONACO

The closest that drivers of the 21st century can get to their forebears is to race at Monaco. Monza has similar longevity, but change has been less in the principality.

Monaco is like no other circuit. For starters, it has been the only street circuit since the dropping of Adelaide from the calendar after 1995, but the difference between street circuits is greater than their tailor-made brethren, so it really is stand-alone.

Take the land on which it is built: it's steep and there's precious little space for the circuit to thread its way along the narrow streets. Indeed, when the race isn't in town and the barriers have been packed away, it's hard to identify its course. Buildings such as the casino are identifiable, but most flash by in the background when you watch the race. It's a relic of bygone days, but remains a vital part of Formula One for providing historic continuity, something different to the norm

and a welcome dose of glamour.

One of the hardest corners of the lap is the first one, St Devote, approached via the right-arcing start/finish 'straight'. If a driver realises he's got it wrong, he'll have to pray that he can guide his errant car up the escape roads or it will slam into the barriers. Massenet, at the crest of the hill after the steep climb to Casino Square is another tricky turn, but drivers tend to find Monaco easy once they've done a few laps and the days of semi-automatic gearboxes have eased the physical strain of making the 50 gear changes required per lap. Also, there is very little in the way of g-force to endure at this low-speed circuit, leaving them fresh to enjoy the celebrations should they win.

The day it all began: The circuit hosted the first Monaco GP back in 1929, when 'W Williams' won in a Bugatti. Monaco held the second ever round of the World Championship in 1950 when Giuseppe Farina precipitated a first lap accident that took out nine cars. Having been just ahead of it, Juan Manuel Fangio was able to escape for victory for Alfa Romeo.

Do you remember when?: Riccardo Patrese won the race that no-one seemed to want to win in 1982. Victory was set to go to Alain Prost, but he crashed his Renault as drizzle fell with three laps to go. Patrese took over, but spun his Brabham a lap later. This left Didier Pironi in front, until his Ferrari's electrics failed. Andrea de Cesaris ought to have taken the lead at this point, but his Alfa Romeo ran out of fuel, leaving the way clear for Patrese to take it.

What makes it difficult?: Trying to get straightline speed while running with the maximum downforce required to propel the car through the many tight corners. Tyre choice is more critical than most places to get grip.

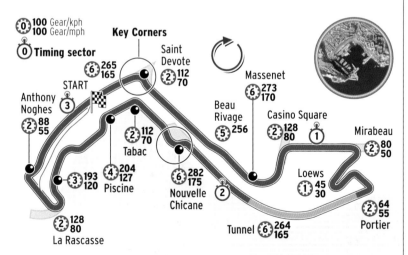

2007 POLE TIME: **Alonso (McLaren)**, 1m15.726s, 98.645mph/158.754kph
2007 FASTEST LAP: **Alonso (McLaren)**, 1m15.284s, 99.242mph/159.715kph

2007 WINNER'S AVERAGE SPEED: 96.655mph/155.551kph
LAP RECORD: **M Schumacher (Ferrari)**, 1m14.439s, 100.373mph/161.527kph, 2004

MONTREAL

Tough on engines and notably hard on the brakes as well, the Circuit Gilles Villeneuve remains a favourite with the fans as it inevitably provides race incident galore.

With walls close to the racing line all of the way around the Montreal circuit, there's always someone hitting them. It usually happens as they exit the final chicane onto the start/finish straight. Even the best drivers get it wrong there, to the extent that the wall they slam into almost at the feet of the people in the grandstand is known as 'champions' wall'.

However, the images of Robert Kubica's accident in last year's Canadian GP were altogether more dramatic. Ironically, it was the fact that he veered off at the place where the barriers are furthest from the track that is considered to have made his crash worse rather than better. To this end, it was recommended that the barrier before the hairpin is moved closer to the track edge and made to run parallel with the circuit. High debris fencing will also have been installed.

Although narrow, this circuit built on an island in the St Laurence River always offers race action. The left-hander ahead of the second corner, the Island hairpin, inevitably sees drivers getting it wrong as they scramble for positions on the opening lap. Then there's always the chance of an outbraking move into the far hairpin or a brave dive up the inside of a rival into the final chicane.

In between these points, though, are testing, twisting yet high-speed sweepers along the north side of the island, where the loss of momentum from slipping off the racing line can lose considerable time, or lead to a meeting with a wall...

INSIDE TRACK

CANADIAN GRAND PRIX

Date:	8 June
Circuit name:	Circuit Gilles Villeneuve
Circuit length:	2.710 miles/4.361km
Number of laps:	70
Telephone:	001 514 350 0000
Website:	www.grandprix.ca

PREVIOUS WINNERS

1998	**Michael Schumacher** FERRARI
1999	**Mika Hakkinen** McLAREN
2000	**Michael Schumacher** FERRARI
2001	**Ralf Schumacher** WILLIAMS
2002	**Michael Schumacher** FERRARI
2003	**Michael Schumacher** FERRARI
2004	**Michael Schumacher** FERRARI
2005	**Kimi Raikkonen** McLAREN
2006	**Fernando Alonso** RENAULT
2007	**Lewis Hamilton** McLAREN

The day it all began: After years of Canada having its grand prix at Mosport Park, Montreal took over in 1978 and Jean-Pierre Jarier led the first 49 laps, running 30s clear. Local hero Gilles Villeneuve took over for Ferrari after Jarier's Lotus broke a brake pipe and went on to lead the final 21 laps . The crowd went mad and the organisers named the new circuit after him.

Do you remember when?: Jean Alesi copied Gilles Villeneuve's celebratory tears when he scored his only grand prix victory here in 1995. Racing for Ferrari, the highly-strung Frenchman had started fifth and done well to climb to second after 18 laps, but the race was clearly going to be won by Michael Schumacher for Benetton, until its gearbox started playing up and he dropped back with 12 laps to go.

What makes it difficult?: With its hairpin, tight corners and chicane, this is a brake-sapping circuit. It's also an engine cooker as more time is spent on full throttle than at any other circuit. Marmots look sweet, but these furry animals appear to have a death wish.

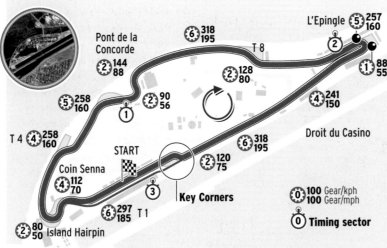

2007 POLE TIME: **Hamilton (McLaren)**, 1m15.707s, 128.865mph/207.389kph

2007 FASTEST LAP: **Alonso (McLaren)**, 1m16.367s, 127.768mph/205.623kph

2007 WINNER'S AVERAGE SPEED: **109.259mph/175.836kph**

LAP RECORD: **Barrichello (Ferrari)**, 1m13.622s, 132.511mph/213.246kph, 2004

MAGNY-COURS

Saved from oblivion by the skin of its teeth, this oh-so-smooth circuit in the middle of the country retains the French GP for now, but a Paris street race beckons.

It seemed last July that it was all over for Magny-Cours. It was set to lose the grand prix, perhaps to Paul Ricard or perhaps to a street race in Paris. Formula One chief Bernie Ecclestone chose not to attend, going instead to Las Vegas to sound out a possible new venue for the US GP instead, saying he wasn't at Magny-Cours as he "doesn't like attending funerals".

With the circuit owners having already removed Magny-Cours from the 2008 Formula One calendar so that they could concentrate on safeguarding its future, things looked black. However, the French motorsport body pushed and before summer was out was rewarded.

So, the drivers are faced once more with the flow of a circuit that they have always liked, even if the spectators haven't. The Grande Courbe, is tricky as it dips to the left, into a crucial corner. This is Estoril, and exit speed is vital from here as it feeds onto the longest straight. Good momentum up here is vital in order to enable drivers to get a slipstream and then try an outbraking manoeuvre into the Adelaide hairpin. This is where the best action happens, and it's safe to say that not all of the moves pay off. Then comes the drivers' favourite stretch, downhill through the Nurburgring esse to the 180 corner and back up the incline through the Imola esse at the top. This is one of the most spectacular corners of the whole season.

INSIDE TRACK

FRENCH GRAND PRIX

Date:	22 June
Circuit name:	Magny-Cours
Circuit length:	2.741 miles/4.411km
Number of laps:	70
Telephone:	00 33 3 86218000
Website:	www.magny-cours.com

PREVIOUS WINNERS

1998	Michael Schumacher FERRARI
1999	Heinz-Harald Frentzen JORDAN
2000	David Coulthard McLAREN
2001	Michael Schumacher FERRARI
2002	Michael Schumacher FERRARI
2003	Ralf Schumacher WILLIAMS
2004	Michael Schumacher FERRARI
2005	Fernando Alonso RENAULT
2006	Michael Schumacher FERRARI
2007	Kimi Raikkonen FERRARI

The day it all began: Although Magny-Cours was a club racing circuit from 1961, it wasn't until 1989 that it became of international calibre, with its first grand prix in 1991 when Nigel Mansell won for Williams after overcoming an early challenge from Alain Prost who led for Ferrari until he was passed not once but twice by the flying Englishman.

Do you remember when?: It rained heavily in 1999 and the race was a lottery as conditions kept changing. Thanks to the deployment of the safety car when the rain was at its heaviest, Jordan's Heinz-Harald Frentzen was able to save sufficient fuel not to have to pit again, thus putting him into the lead with seven laps to go when McLaren's Mika Hakkinen called in for fuel. Electrical failure cost early race leader David Coulthard probable victory for McLaren.

What makes it difficult?: The surface changes more than most according to temperature and tyre degradation can be a factor. With a short pitlane, making a third pitstop is less of a gamble here than elsewhere.

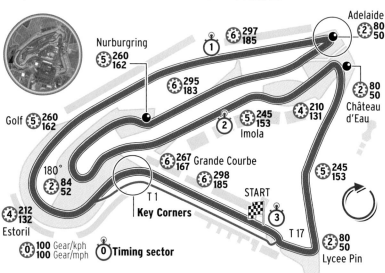

2007 POLE TIME: **Massa (Ferrari)**, 1m15.034s, 131.508mph/211.643kph
2007 FASTEST LAP: **Massa (Ferrari)**, 1m16.099s, 129.661mph/203.721kph

2007 WINNER'S AVERAGE SPEED: 126.586mph/200.958kph
LAP RECORD: **M Schumacher (Ferrari)**, 1m15.377s, 130.910mph/210.669kph, 2004

SILVERSTONE

Hamiltonmania filled Silverstone last year and there is every expectation that the McLaren man will be bringing the fans through the turnstiles again.

Silverstone's crowd changed its spots last year when it opened its doors to thousands of 'first-time buyers' who came to see what Lewis Hamilton was all about. Such was the excitement of the meeting that you can be sure that they will be back again this year.

Yet, for all this euphoria, the future of the British GP remains a tiresome battle, with Bernie Ecclestone taking potshots at the circuit for failing to match the facilities seen at the new tracks in Turkey, China and Bahrain. Silverstone's owners - the British Racing Drivers' Club - also seems to be in perpetual civil war as it decides how best to develop the circuit, with plans to build a pit and paddock complex between Club and Abbey being Ecclestone's preferred choice.

The parties are only united when agreeing that the whole matter could be resolved if the British government followed the path of others and invested in the circuit and, to whit, in the world-leading British motorsport industry.

Disregard the politics, though, and Silverstone still remains one of the best tracks visited, for it allows real racing. The first corner, Copse, is still tricky, but it's the Becketts sweepers that the drivers all talk about. they're downright difficult and definitely the place to watch from in qualifying. Stowe is not as fast as it used to be, nor Club, but a good exit from either offers a chance to pass into the bnext corner, Vale and Abbey respectively.

INSIDE TRACK

BRITISH GRAND PRIX

Date:	**6 July**
Circuit name:	**Silverstone**
Circuit length:	**3.194 miles/5.140km**
Number of laps:	**60**
Telephone:	**01327 857271**
Website:	**www.silverstone-circuit.co.uk**

PREVIOUS WINNERS	
1998	**Michael Schumacher** FERRARI
1999	**David Coulthard** McLAREN
2000	**David Coulthard** McLAREN
2001	**Mika Hakkinen** McLAREN
2002	**Michael Schumacher** FERRARI
2003	**Rubens Barrichello** FERRARI
2004	**Michael Schumacher** FERRARI
2005	**Juan Pablo Montoya** McLAREN
2006	**Fernando Alonso** RENAULT
2007	**Kimi Raikkonen** FERRARI

The day it all began: The Second World War was over, this airfield no longer essential, so it was turned into a race venue, hosting its first grand prix in 1948. This was won by Luigi Villoresi in a Maserati, with Giuseppe Farina winning the first ever World Championship round in 1950 as Alfa Romeo cleaned up. Team-mate Luigi Fagioli had led from the start, but Farina took over and triumphed ahead of his fellow Italian, with British driver Reg Parnell third.

Do you remember when?: Michael Schumacher won the 1998 British GP despite taking the finish in the pits. Michael had passed title rival Mika Hakkinen for the lead with 10 laps to go. However, he had passed Alex Wurz under a yellow flag and was served with notification of a stop-go penalty. You have to do this within three laps, which he did, except that the third lap was the final one, so he took the chequered flag en route to his pit.

What makes it difficult?: With its fast, open sweeps, aerodynamic efficiency is vital, as is high-speed stability for the Becketts esses.

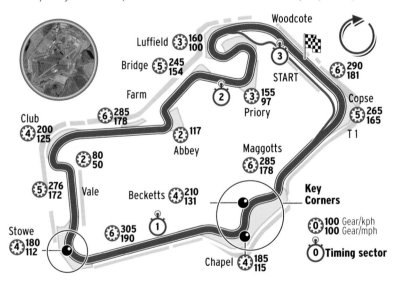

Woodcote

Luffield ③ 160 / 100

Bridge ⑤ 245 / 154

Farm

START

3

⑥ 290 / 181

② 155 / 97

Priory

Copse

⑤ 265 / 165

T 1

Club ④ 200 / 125

⑥ 285 / 178

② 117

② 80 / 50

Abbey

Maggotts ⑥ 285 / 178

⑤ 276 / 172

Vale

Becketts ④ 210 / 131

Key Corners

⓪ 100 Gear/kph / 100 Gear/mph

Stowe ④ 180 / 112

⑥ 305 / 190

①

⓪ Timing sector

Chapel ④ 185 / 115

2007 POLE TIME: **Hamilton (McLaren)**, 1m19.997s, 143.735mph/231.320kph	2007 WINNER'S AVERAGE SPEED: 138.364mph/222.676kph
2007 FASTEST LAP: **Raikkonen (Ferrari)**, 1m20.638s, 142.548mph/229.409kph	LAP RECORD: **M Schumacher (Ferrari)**, 1m18.739s, 146.059mph/235.048kph, 2004

HOCKENHEIM

After a year on the sidelines as its alternation with the Nurburgring kicked in, Hockenheim is back, with its heat, humidity and noisy stadium.

Hockenheim is back on board for 2008, but it's not the solid gold venue it once was. Financial problems set in a couple of years ago and were then compounded when it was decided by the FIA that Germany ought no longer host two grands prix per year - with the one at the Nurburgring under the courtesy title of the European GP.

There was never any justification for it, however popular Michael Schumacher was. Hockenheim has survived, though, and celebrated its 75th anniversary last year.

Hockenheim is not the circuit it once was, with much of its length hacked off for 2002, with most of the lengthy loop through the forest removed. Key to the character of what remains is the stadium section when the track snakes past lofty grandstands full of fans armed with airhorns. The first corner, the Nordkurve, still claims a scalp or two on the first lap, but bunching also occurs at the second corner, the tight right onto the back section.

Then comes the bend with the longest name in Formula One: Hochgeschwindigkeits Kurve, an arcing left that takes the drivers up to one of the best passing spots, the Spitzkehre. This is a hairpin built on what used to be the return leg through the forest and, from here, the cars have to navigate a right kink, a tight left, another right and a short straight before reaching the stadium where the fans enjoy a great view of the final five corners.

INSIDE TRACK

GERMAN GRAND PRIX

Date:	20 July
Circuit name:	Hockenheim
Circuit length:	2.842 miles/4.574km
Number of laps:	67
Telephone:	00 49 6205 95005
Website:	www.hockenheimring.de

PREVIOUS WINNERS

1997	Gerhard Berger	BENETTON
1998	Mika Hakkinen	McLAREN
1999	Eddie Irvine	FERRARI
2000	Rubens Barrichello	FERRARI
2001	Ralf Schumacher	WILLIAMS
2002	Michael Schumacher	FERRARI
2003	Juan Pablo Montoya	WILLIAMS
2004	Michael Schumacher	FERRARI
2005	Fernando Alonso	RENAULT
2006	Michael Schumacher	FERRARI

The day it all began: Hockenheim seems enshrined as the home of the German GP, but it is really the Nurburgring that deserves to hold that title as it was the country's premier circuit from 1927. Hockenheim didn't host the German GP until 1970, and that was a one-off until Niki Lauda's near death at the Nurburgring in 1976 handed the race to Hockenheim, with the Nurburgring only returning in 1984.

Do you remember when?: The 2000 GP remains one of the oddest when Rubens Barrichello took his maiden win, from 18th on the grid. McLaren had been in control, but a disenchanted Mercedes employee invaded the track and brought out the safety car. Mika Hakkinen pitted and, in an instant, Barrichello's Ferrari had cut the lead to nothing. Then rain fell, on half of the circuit, and Hakkinen pitted for wets. Barrichello didn't and came to win.

What makes it difficult?: The Einfahrt Parabolika, is probably the trickiest, as the field can bunch here on the first lap, meaning that drivers must be extra careful not to hit or be hit.

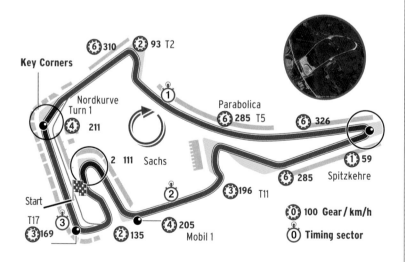

Key Corners

Nordkurve Turn 1 — 211
2 111 Sachs
Start
T17
169
135
205 Mobil 1
196 T11
285 T5 Parabolica
310
93 T2
1
326
59
285 Spitzkehre
100 Gear / km/h
Timing sector

2006 POLE TIME: Raikkonen (McLaren), 1m14.070s, 138.129mph/222.297kph
2006 FASTEST LAP: M Schumacher (Ferrari), 1m16.357s, 134.005mph/215.661kph
2006 WINNER'S AVERAGE SPEED: 130.045mph/209.288kph
LAP RECORD: Raikkonen, 1m14.917s, 138.685mph/223.192kph

HUNGARORING

Sunshine and packed grandstands and hillsides make the Hungaroring look out, but an almost total lack of scope for overtaking leads to an annual procession.

Looking at the positives first, the Hungaroring offers some of the finest vantage points of any grand prix circuit as the track flows along one side of a valley, down into the dip, along the other side and back again.

Yet the Hungaroring offers as little scope for overtaking as Monaco. Drivers are able to gain a place or two if they get the first corner right on the opening lap, and perhaps pick up another place, or lose one, at Turn 2, but the tight exit from the hairpin onto the start/finish straight, Turn 14, makes it almost impossible to replicate this on any other lap of the race.

The drivers find the circuit fun to drive, especially the series of esses along the far side of the valley - Turn 6 to Turn 10 - but their best hope for overtaking is for the driver in front to make a mistake. In days of old, such an opportunity would have come when a driver missed a gear, but semi-automatic clutches have removed that variable, more's the pity.

One other place that can provide an overtaking option is if a driver is running on worn tyres - something that happens a lot at the Hungaroring due to the high ambient temperatures - and runs wide at the uphill Turn 4, which is how Takuma Sato pulled off a blinder there last year before having to throw out the anchors to slow enough to take the right-hand hairpin onto the level plain from Turn 5.

INSIDE TRACK

HUNGARIAN GRAND PRIX

Date:	3 August
Circuit name:	Hungaroring
Circuit length:	2.722 miles/4.381km
Number of laps:	70
Telephone:	00 36 2 844 1861
Website:	www.hungaroring.hu

PREVIOUS WINNERS

1998	Michael Schumacher FERRARI
1999	Mika Hakkinen McLAREN
2000	Mika Hakkinen McLAREN
2001	Michael Schumacher FERRARI
2002	Rubens Barrichello FERRARI
2003	Fernando Alonso RENAULT
2004	Michael Schumacher FERRARI
2005	Kimi Raikkonen McLAREN
2006	Jenson Button HONDA
2007	Lewis Hamilton McLAREN

The day it all began: The Hungaroring opened in 1986 and had a grand prix in its first year, won by Nelson Piquet for Williams after a great battle with Ayrton Senna's Lotus on a circuit packed with 200,000 spectators. Hungary had hosted a grand prix before, in downtown Nepliget Park in 1936, with Tazio Nuvolari winning for Alfa Romeo.

Do you remember when?: Fernando Alonso scored his first grand prix win here in 2003. He'd finished second in Spain, but the manner of his victory in sky high temperatures shocked even those who tipped him for success, as pole was converted into the lead out of the first corner ahead of Mark Webber's Jaguar, which faded, and he went on to blitz the field, finishing 17s ahead of Kimi Raikkonen's McLaren. This broke Bruce McLaren's long-standing record to become the youngest grand prix winner ever at 22 years and 26 days.

What makes it difficult?: This is a high downforce circuit that is hard on tyres and cooling is always an issue due to soaring ambient temperatures in August.

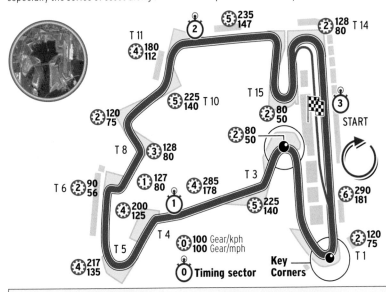

T 11
④ 180 112

⑤ 235 147 (2)   (2) 128 80 T 14

② 120 75

⑤ 225 140 T 10   T 15   ③
② 80 50   START

T 8   ③ 128 80   ② 80 50

T 3

T 6 ② 90 56   ① 127 80   ④ 285 178   ⑥ 290 181

④ 200 125   ①   ⑤ 225 140

T 4   ② 120 75

T 5   ⓪ 100 Gear/kph 100 Gear/mph   **Key Corners**   T 1

④ 217 135   ⓪ **Timing sector**

2007 POLE TIME: **Hamilton (McLaren),**
1m19.781s, 122.826mph/197.670kph
2007 FASTEST LAP: **Raikkonen (Ferrari),**
1m20.047s, 122.428mph/197.029kph

2007 WINNER'S AVERAGE SPEED:
119.239mph/191.897kph
LAP RECORD: **M Schumacher (Ferrari)**
1m19.071s, 123.828mph/199.461kph, 2004

VALENCIA

This year will be a treat for street racing fans, as Monaco is being joined by new tracks in Singapore and here in Spain around the port at Valencia.

Just as Germany and Italy were stopped from hosting two grands prix a year, with the European GP allowing the Nurburgring a race to accompany Hockenheim's and the San Marino GP doing likewise for Imola and Monza, so Spain gains a bonus race, to be called the European GP. This flies in the face of the shift of grands prix from Europe to points further around the globe. However, it is a direct result of Fernando Alonso's world championship successes. The machinations of the deal triggered some furious headlines, though, as it had been intimated that the deal was dependent on the president of the regional government remaining in power in forthcoming elections. This was denied

and the furore died down when they were voted back in anyway.

Valencia has been awash with yachting as the host port for the America's Cup extravaganza. There is an established circuit popular for Formula One testing just outside Valencia, yet, wanting to make the most of the regeneration of its port and the building of its image, this go-ahead city found the money to build a street circuit.

The 25-turn circuit lay-out runs around the harbour area. Amazingly for a street circuit, the main straight is so long that the cars are expected to top 200mph, which is faster than they manage on many purpose-built road circuits.

INSIDE TRACK

EUROPEAN GRAND PRIX

Date:	**24 August**
Circuit name:	**Valencia**
Circuit length:	**3.401 miles/5.473km**
Number of laps:	**TBC**
Website:	**www.formulaunovalencia.com**

What's new?: The Valencia circuit will be the first new street circuit since Phoenix hit the Formula One scene back in 1991 as the then home of the US GP.

What's the deal?: FOM have signed for the next seven years.

Who is behind the race?: There's a strong sporting involvement as the Valmor Group who did the deal to the host the race includes the president of the Villareal football club, Fernando Roig, and former motorcycle racer Jorge Martinez Aspar.

What did it all cost?: The city of Valencia spent more than £1.35 billion improving its facilities and its port area for the America's Cup. With its own street race and also the Volvo Ocean Race passing through in 2008, the city is reaping the dividends of its investment, in recognition as much as financial returns. The new circuit will also make use of an old railway area and thus help tidy up a delapidated area of the city.

Who designed it?: Why, the ubiquitous circuit architect Hermann Tilke, of course.

What makes it difficult?: Going to any new circuit for the first time provides problems aplenty. There's a lack of track knowledge. There's no idea of the surface quality which obviously affects tyre wear. The surface takes a long time to 'rubber in'. Then there's the eternal compromise that street circuits always throw up: how to balance the need for high wing angle to help the car through the tight corners yet need little wing for making the most of the straights.

Circuit map

- ② 100 T 2
- ③ 139 T 5
- T 7 ⑥ 298
- T 8
- ③ 163
- ⑥ 307 T 3
- ④ 228
- T 1
- T 10
- ⑥ 283
- T 11 ⑤ 253
- ④ 218 / 135
- ⑥ 310
- START
- ③ 171
- ② 98
- T 21
- T 25
- ⓪ 100 Gear/kph / 100 Gear/mph
- ⑥ 323
- T 15
- T 12
- T 17
- ⑥ 312
- ④ 196
- ③ 180 / 112

SPA-FRANCORCHAMPS

The drivers love it, the fans love it and it makes fabulous TV, so it's a mystery why Spa has spent recent years dotting in and out of the World Championship.

Spa is a town famous for its mineral springs. Francorchamps is a village up the road in the rolling Ardennes hills. Together, they are united as one of the greatest grand prix circuits ever. Spa-Francorchamps may be seen as a relic, but its continual reshaping keeps it within contemporary safety moves and yet does everyone the favour of keeping its soul by offering the drivers a challenge to get their teeth into.

It's tricky, with the cars reaching the La Source hairpin only seconds after powering away from the grid. What follows can fail to excite only the dead, as it's the drop to Eau Rouge, a magnificent left-right at the foot of the dip before the cars are fired up again and the drivers have to wrestle them through the left-hand kink, Raidillion.

After the long climb to Les Combes, where the original circuit dropped into the neighbouring valley, the track falls away again, with the double-apex, downhill Pouhon a real challenge. After the Fagnes esses, Stavelot marks the start of the climb back up to the pits, with the Bus Stop chicane seemingly ever being reprofiled.

The best change recently has been the new pits complex, as the previous ones were not a great deal better than the cramped garages offered at Interlagos.

If the circuit isn't tricky enough in its own right, there's always the possibility of rain, and always the further possibility that it might hit only one end of the circuit...

INSIDE TRACK

BELGIAN GRAND PRIX

Date:	7 September
Circuit name:	Spa-Francorchamps
Circuit length:	4.352 miles/7.004km
Number of laps:	44
Telephone:	00 32 8727 5138
Website:	www.spa-francorchamps.be

PREVIOUS WINNERS

1996	**Michael Schumacher** FERRARI
1997	**Michael Schumacher** FERRARI
1998	**Damon Hill** JORDAN
1999	**David Coulthard** McLAREN
2000	**Mika Hakkinen** McLAREN
2001	**Michael Schumacher** FERRARI
2002	**Michael Schumacher** FERRARI
2004	**Kimi Raikkonen** McLAREN
2005	**Kimi Raikkonen** McLAREN
2007	**Kimi Raikkonen** FERRARI

The day it all began: The original 9-mile form of this circuit was used in 1924 and hosted the first Belgian GP in 1925 when Antonio Ascari was first home for Alfa Romeo. It was Juan Manuel Fangio who won its first World Championship event in 1950, for Alfa Romeo. Emphasising how thin the field was, only 14 cars turned up and Fangio fought past team-mate Farina to win.

Do you remember when?: A year after his Formula One debut here, Michael Schumacher scored his first win in 1992. He started behind Nigel Mansell and Ayrton Senna, but what had looked like a fourth place finish was converted into a win was the timing of his change to slick tyres, something that had been made obvious when he ran off the track but rejoined behind Benetton team-mate Martin Brundle and noticed that his wet weather tyres were blistering, so pitted, getting the timing spot on.

What makes it difficult?: The kerbs at the chicanes need to be attacked. Carrying speed through the downhill Pouhon corner is a test, too, as is the down-and-up Eau Rouge corner.

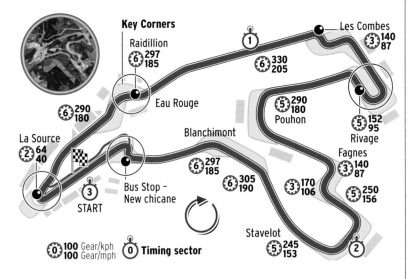

Key Corners

Raidillion 6 297/185

Les Combes 3 140/87

6 330/205

6 290/180

Eau Rouge

5 290/180 Pouhon

5 152/95 Rivage

La Source 2 64/40

Blanchimont

Fagnes 3 140/87

3 START

Bus Stop – New chicane

6 297/185

6 305/190

3 170/106

5 250/156

0 100/100 Gear/kph Gear/mph

0 Timing sector

Stavelot 5 245/153

2

2007 POLE TIME: Raikkonen (Ferrari),
1m45.994s, 146.618mph/235.947kph
2007 FASTEST LAP: Massa (Ferrari),
1m48.036s, 145.051mph/233.437kph

2007 WINNER'S AVERAGE SPEED:
142.432mph/229.223kph
LAP RECORD: Massa (Ferrari), 1m48.036s,
145.051mph/233.437kph, 2007

MONZA

The chicanes are a nuisance, especially on the opening lap, but the high-speed nature of this Italian circuit still conjures images of its glorious past.

After it abandoned its banking in the 1950s, Monza was the home of the ultimate slipstreaming packs hunting together and against each other down the long straights before bursting into the corners. Then came the chicanes, braking the flow of this great Italian circuit and with it the nature of the circuit was transformed. Overtaking manoeuvres take far more planning now.

Still, though, Monza's parkland setting is magnificent, and even the circuit's slightly run-down infrastructure fine in the late summer sun. There continue to be little nips and tucks every year, with the gravel traps at the second chicane being replaced by a tarmac run-off area last year. However, the biggest change of all is the one that local mayor has been fighting against. This is the closure of the circuit, something that the environmentalists have been seeking for years. His aim is to have the royal park declared a national monument.

Race fans the world over will be praying that he succeeds as where would we all be without our annual fix of 22 cars trying to fit through the first chicane after their blast down the main straight from the grid? We'd miss, too, the challenge the drivers face at the Lesmo, their braking into and acceleration out of the Variante Ascari. Most of all, though, racing fans would feel short-changed without the sight of Formula One cars tackling the mighty final corner, the Parabolica.

INSIDE TRACK

ITALIAN GRAND PRIX

Date:	**14 September**
Circuit name:	**Monza**
Circuit length:	**3.600 miles/5.793km**
Number of laps:	**53**
Telephone:	**00 39 39 24821**
Website:	**www.monzanet.it**

PREVIOUS WINNERS

1998	**Michael Schumacher** FERRARI
1999	**Heinz-Harald Frentzen** JORDAN
2000	**Michael Schumacher** FERRARI
2001	**Juan Pablo Montoya** WILLIAMS
2002	**Rubens Barrichello** FERRARI
2003	**Michael Schumacher** FERRARI
2004	**Rubens Barrichello** FERRARI
2005	**Juan Pablo Montoya** McLAREN
2006	**Michael Schumacher** FERRARI
2007	**Fernando Alonso** McLAREN

The day it all began: As it began all back in 1922, Monza is one of the oldest continually used circuits, taking over from Brescia as the home of the Italian GP. Pietro Bordino won for Fiat that year, with Alfa Romeo's Giuseppe Farina first home on its World Championship debut in 1950. Alberto Ascari gave Ferrari hope of a win on home soil, but engine failure and then Juan Manuel Fangio dropping out with a broken gearbox left Farina free to win.

Do you remember when?: The closest massed finish ever came in 1971 when Peter Gethin nosed his BRM to the front of a five-car pack. He had led, but dropped to the back of the lead pack, only to overhaul Ronnie Peterson who led the penultimate lap for March, Francois Cevert, Mike Hailwood and his own team-mate Howden Ganley on the sprint to the line. The first four were covered by 0.18s.

What makes it difficult?: This circuit presses engines hard. With low downforce the choice set-up because of the long straights, drivers find their cars nervous to drive.

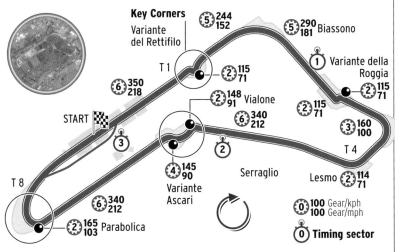

Key Corners

Variante del Rettifilo

T 1

350
218

244
152

290
181 Biassono

Variante della Roggia

115
71

115
71

148
91 Vialone

115
71

340
212

160
100

T 4

START

3

2

2

145
90

Variante Ascari

Serraglio

Lesmo

114
71

T 8

340
212

165
103 Parabolica

100 Gear/kph
100 Gear/mph

Timing sector

2007 POLE TIME: **Alonso (McLaren),**
1m21.997s, 158.055mph/254.365kph
2007 FASTEST LAP: **Alonso (McLaren),**
1m22.871s, 156.402mph/251.705kph

2007 WINNER'S AVERAGE SPEED:
145.460mph/234.096kph
LAP RECORD: **Barrichello (Ferrari),**
1m21.046s, 159.899mph/257.321kph, 2004

SINGAPORE

Not only is Singapore new to Formula One, but it will hold its race after dark, not just as it's so hot during the day, but so that it's held when Europe is awake.

When Bernie Ecclestone puts pressure on the European circuits, this is just the sort of development he has in mind.

As one of south-east Asia's commercial hubs, Singapore's corporate power make it an attractive proposition. Throw in the fact that its backdrop for a street race is startling and you can see its appeal. Finally, and this is the bit that Bernie likes, it keeps neighbouring Malaysia on its toes, stopping it from feeling too content.

Hermann Tilke was the man behind the Singapore circuit's lay-out. Being in the city centre, its shape has been dictated by the lie of the land, but it looks to be unusually fast and open for a street circuit.

The circuit runs in an anti-clockwise direction, with a run through a water-front park before turning right off Republic Boulevard and onto Raffles Boulevard to kink right past some of Singapore's fanciest hotels, even taking in an underpass at speeds expected to top 200mph.

A tighter section follows, before the cars power past the old colonial government buildings and the Padang sports fields. One of the most spectacular sections is where the track runs across the arched Anderson Bridge and then turns sharp left onto the above-water Esplanade Drive.

The home section is next, after a tight right onto Raffles Drive, with a final right-left esse past a huge grandstand then a left-right under it.

Previous experience necessary: Colin Syn, who has overseen the project, raced in on the streets of Singapore in the early 1970s.

Built in a hurry: The first construction work began in the Marina Bay area at the start of September 2007, just over a year before its maiden grand prix, with the pit buildings.

Saving the trees: It would have been easier to chop trees down to fit in the circuit, but many are considered sacred and so had to be saved.

With a little help: Alert to the prestige brought by hosting a grand prix, the Singapore government put up 60% of the budget.

Built large: The grandstand on Raffles Avenue can accommodate 26,000 spectators. It is also used for aquatic events on Marina Bay.

Running in the night: Like the neighbouring Malaysian GP, the Singapore GP will be held after nightfall, but specially-developed flood lighting will make it seem like daylight to the drivers. This was tested extensively at Paul Ricard in France, with Nelson Piquet Jr conducting much of the mileage.

Watch out for: The Singapore Flyer, which is an even larger version of the London Eye. This giant Ferris Wheel will be located on the inside of the final corner and offer a stunning view of the circuit from its rotating cabins.

What makes it difficult?: Street circuits are always bumpy and new ones even more so. They also take time for rubber to be impregnated into the circuit by use and so are unusually slippery. Temperatures will be high and humidity too, bringing the risk of torrential tropical rain storms.

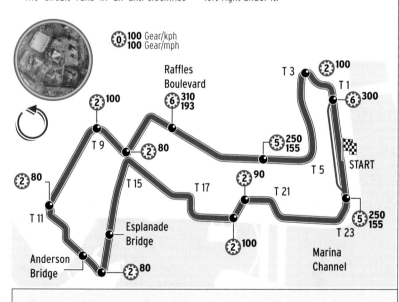

FUJI SPEEDWAY

There was so much spray in last year's race that many fans will be getting their first sight of the much revised Fuji Speedway this time around.

Older Formula One viewers will remember Fuji Speedway when it flitted onto the calendar for 1976 and 1977 before disappearing again following the death of a marshal and a spectator who he was trying to move from a prohibited zone. British fans in particular are kept in mind of the circuit on the slopes of Japan's sacred volcano by reruns of James Hunt claiming the third place that he required to be crowned world champion in 1976. However, it was amazing that Formula One stayed away from Japan until it started returning in 1987, to Suzuka, and stayed away from Toyota-owned Fuji Speedway until last year.

Now that it's back, with an alternation deal starting with Honda-owned Suzuka hosting the Japanese GP in 2009, the circuit offers drivers a mix of fast and slow.

The run down the main straight is definitely fast, the right-hand hairpin at its end definitely slow. In the dry, it should offer scope for overtaking. Dipping gently downhill, the track runs towards 100R, a tricky corner that requires commitment.

Everything slows down for the hairpin behind the paddock that follows, then opens out again for the run to the Dunlop Corner. the insertion of a chicane here and, even more critically, the slow Netz corner that follows ensures that cars don't carry much speed into the final corner, Panasonic Corner, so that they don't take this onto the long start/finish straight.

INSIDE TRACK

JAPANESE GRAND PRIX

Date:	12 October
Circuit name:	Fuji Speedway
Circuit length:	2.852 miles/4.563km
Number of laps:	67
Telephone:	00 81 550 781234
Website:	www.fujispeedway.jp/english

PREVIOUS WINNERS

1976	**Mario Andretti**	LOTUS
1977	**James Hunt**	McLAREN
2007	**Lewis Hamilton**	McLAREN

The day it all began: Back in 1965, the Fuji Speedway opened for business, but it was a very different proposition as its original circuit layout was one mile longer and included a long, steeply-banked right-hander as its first corner. This was cut straight into the mountainside, as were the terraced seating above it, with the track only coming out of this banked section after going through 180 degrees, even then tightening and feeding on even more to the right before curving left to the point at which the hairpin that replaced it fed down towards the second corner..

Do you remember when?: James Hunt wrapped up the 1976 title here in conditions only marginally less torrential than last year's encounter, thus becoming the first British World Champion since Jackie Stewart did so in 1973. With Niki Lauda unable to blink because of facial burns, the Ferrari driver pulled out after two laps. Hunt then led through to lap 61, but first Patrick Depailler and then Mario Andretti took over. After a late tyre stop, Hunt worked his way back to third, which was just enough.

What makes it difficult?: The long start/finish straight makes engineers want to send their cars out with a low wing angle, but they also need wing to help them through the tighter corners . Also, the weather can be a little on the wet side. Just ask Lewis Hamilton...

Panasonic Corner
13th corner
Netz Corner
Dunlop Corner
300R
START
Main Grandstand
Hairpin Corner
1st Corner Grandstand
Coca-Cola Corner
100R

0 Gear

2007 POLE TIME: Hamilton (McLaren), 1m25.368s, 120.270mph/193.556kph	**2007 WINNER'S AVERAGE SPEED:** 94.439mph/151.985kph
2007 FASTEST LAP: Hamilton (McLaren), 1m28.193s, 115.736mph/186.259kph	**LAP RECORD: Hamilton (McLaren),** 1m28.193s, 115.736mph/186.259kph, 2007

SHANGHAI

It's massive in every way, with space to overtake at many of the corners. However, we all know that it's just a little tight when drivers come into the pits...

Television has a habit of making circuits look smaller and flatter than they really are. In the case of Shanghai, there's little gradient to talk about, save for the gentle climb from Turn 1 to Turn 2 and the drop back to the starting level by Turn 3.

What is deceptive, though, is the sheer scale of the place, for the facilities are outsize, vast, even humungous. The track is longer than most and certainly wider. Yet, it's the buildings that are from another league, with the two wing-shaped bridges over the start finish straight, balancing on the main grandstand on one side and the top of towers at either end of the pit complex on the other being roughly four stories high at their deepest.

The circuit is tricky from the outset, with Turns 1 to 3 keeping the drivers on their toes. they have to work, too, through the long left and right and left again behind the paddock. There is a near replica of the first three corners at the far point of the circuit, with the final part of this unwinding onto the back straight which is the longest of all. At the end of this is the hairpin, with the best spot for overtaking coming at turn in, but it's bumpy and tricky, making many a driver overshoot before coming back onto the track to try again.

If the rain last year didn't match that at the previous week's Japanese GP, rain is always a threat as autumn sets in. And there's that gravel trap at pit entry.

INSIDE TRACK

CHINESE GRAND PRIX

Date:	**19 October**
Circuit name:	**Shanghai International Circuit**
Circuit length:	**3.390 miles/5.450km**
Number of laps:	**57**
Telephone:	**00 86 2162520000**
Website:	**www.f1china.com.cn**

PREVIOUS WINNERS	
2004	**Rubens Barrichello** FERRARI
2005	**Fernando Alonso** RENAULT
2006	**Michael Schumacher** FERRARI
2007	**Kimi Raikkonen** FERRARI

The day it all began: It was in the autumn of 2004 that the Formula One circus arrived at the Shanghai International Circuit for the first time and it's safe to say that everyone was blown away by its sheer scale. The drivers loved it, and none more so than Rubens Barrichello who stuck his Ferrari on pole position. With team-mate Michael Schumacher starting from the back after falling off in his one permitted flying lap, Rubens led all the way, save for Jenson Button, who twice pitted later, leading fleetingly for BAR. Button was just 1s down at the finish.

Do you remember when?: Michael Schumacher scored the last of his 91 grand prix wins here in 2006. He still had two races to go in his 16-year Formula One career, but his run to victory was the last time he'd experience the top step of the podium and came after he caught and passed the Renaults of Fernando Alonso and Giancarlo Fisichella in the wet, albeit with the Italian handing him the lead by sliding wide as he exited his second pit stop.

What makes it difficult?: The complex of Turns 1 to 3 is just that, complex, as it rises and falls and keeps turning one way and then back the other through its course. The hairpin at the end of the long back straight is also notably bumpy at just the point at which drivers hit the brakes. And there's considerable pollution.

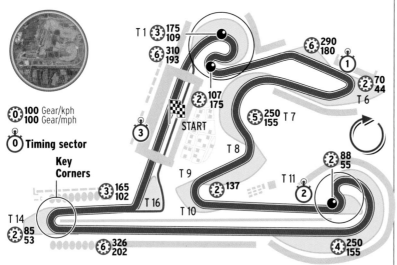

T 1 ③ 175 / 109
⑥ 310 / 193
⑥ 290 / 180
①
② 70 / 44
T 6
② 107 / 175
⑤ 250 / 155 T 7

⓪ 100 Gear/kph
⓪ 100 Gear/mph

⓪ Timing sector

Key Corners

③ 165 / 102
T 16
T 14
② 85 / 53
⑥ 326 / 202

③
START
T 8
T 9
T 10
② 137
T 11
②
② 88 / 55
④ 250 / 155

2007 POLE TIME: **Hamilton (McLaren)**,
1m35.908s, 127.247mph/204.784kph
2007 FASTEST LAP: **Massa (Ferrari)**,
1M37.454s, 125.120mph/201.362kph

2007 WINNER'S AVERAGE SPEED:
116.088mph/186.826kph
LAP RECORD: **M Schumacher (Ferrari)**
1m32.238s, 132.202mph/212.749kph, 2004

INTERLAGOS

This rough-at-the-edges Brazilian circuit has always been great to visit, thanks to the fans' passion, but it's its place at the end of the calendar that adds the spice.

If Formula One was to lose Interlagos, not only would the world championship lose its foothold in South America, but it would lose more of its romance. Much as Ferrari lovers tell you that Ferrari is Formula One, so Formula One needs the Brazilian fans for without them the season would lose one of its special ingredients. Sure, Interlagos doesn't meet the standards or either the made-to-measure super tracks or even the norm of the established European tracks, but it's awash with history and passion. And, not to be missed out from this, it's a serious challenge for the drivers.

From the very first corner, Curva 1, with its blind entry and apex on a crest, the lap offers challenges aplenty. The cars then drop, accelerating again, to the foot of the compression that is the Senna S before the drivers fire them through Curva do Sol for the blast down to Descida do Lago. This double left points the cars back up to Ferra Dura, where the drivers have to work hard again to keep off the bumps and yet keep a rhythm through the lefts and rights that follow before accelerating hard through Junçao onto the long, long, curving blast onto the start/finish straight. Even this is daunting with high walls on either side making it something of a concrete tunnel.

The downside to all of this? That'll be the gunpoint robberies that abound in Sao Paulo, with the teams being a target for their laptops and snazzy watches.

INSIDE TRACK

BRAZILIAN GRAND PRIX

Date:	2 November
Circuit name:	Interlagos
Circuit length:	2.667 miles/4.292km
Number of laps:	71
Telephone:	00 55 11 813 5775
Website:	www.interlagos.com

PREVIOUS WINNERS	
1998	Mika Hakkinen McLAREN
1999	Mika Hakkinen McLAREN
2000	Michael Schumacher FERRARI
2001	David Coulthard McLAREN
2002	Michael Schumacher FERRARI
2003	Giancarlo Fisichella JORDAN
2004	Juan Pablo Montoya WILLIAMS
2005	Juan Pablo Montoya McLAREN
2006	Felipe Massa FERRARI
2007	Kimi Raikkonen FERRARI

The day it all began: Opened in 1940, this circuit built in the Sao Paulo suburbs hosted a non-championship F1 race won by Brabham's Carlos Reutemann in 1972, but is was hometown hero Emerson Fittipaldi who won the first World Championship race there in 1973. He arrived having won the first round and he and Lotus team-mate Ronnie Peterson qualified well clear and all it took was for Emerson to jump the pole-sitting Swede, which he did, leading all the way to victory, with Peterson crashing out.

Do you remember when?: Ayrton Senna won his home race, at the eighth time of asking, in 1991. Racing for McLaren, he had 27 wins to his name since he broke his duck in Portugal for Lotus in 1985. But his home race had been a catalogue of disasters. Until this time, when Ayrton stuck his car on pole and led every lap.

What makes it difficult?: Bumps and constant changes of gradient make this a very physical circuit. The blind entry to the Senna S is tricky. As are parts of the circuit where water runs in streams after a downpour.

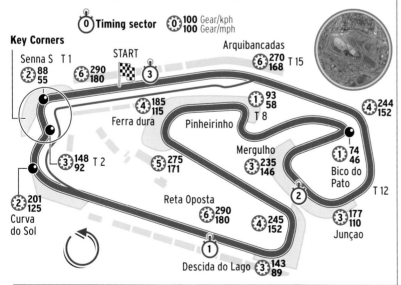

Key Corners

- Timing sector ⓞ
- 100 Gear/kph
- 100 Gear/mph

Senna S T 1
② 88 55
⑥ 290 180
START
③
④ 185 115
Ferra dura
③ 148 92 T 2
② 201 125 Curva do Sol
⑤ 275 171
Reta Oposta
⑥ 290 180
④ 245 152
Pinheirinho
Mergulho
③ 235 146
① 93 58 T 8
Arquibancadas
⑥ 270 168 T 15
④ 244 152
① 74 46 Bico do Pato
③ 177 110 Junçao
T 12
②
① Descida do Lago ③ 143 89

2007 POLE TIME: **Massa (Ferrari), 1m11.931s, 133.978mph/215.618kph**
2007 FASTEST LAP: **Raikkonen (Ferrari), 1m12.445s, 133.028mph/214.088kph**

2007 WINNER'S AVERAGE SPEED: **129.228mph/207.973kph**
LAP RECORD: **Montoya (Williams), 1m 11.473s, 134.867mph/217.038kph, 2004**

REVIEW OF THE 2007 SEASON

This was the season that had it all and, when it came to politics and alleged spying, too much. The battle for the world title was a belter, though, as the final scores of 110, 109, 109 gives lie, with Kimi Raikkonen squeaking through for Ferrari. It wasn't always pretty, but Formula One was never out of the news.

Anyone watching the ease with which Kimi Raikkonen got his career as a Ferrari driver off to a winning start in Australia would have been a fool to think anyone else would be the 2007 World Champion. The fact that he went to the final race ranked third showed just how things can change over the course of 17 grands prix.

It was a year of Ferrari versus a resurgent McLaren, but sadly it was just as busy off the track and the season was overshadowed by the spying scandal that erupted when one of McLaren's design team was found in possession of Ferrari documentation that was

alleged to have been sent to him by a disgruntled member of Ferrari's team hierarchy. It was vicious and the only winners were the lawyers and the FIA for the $100m it fined McLaren, as well as deleting all their points towards the constructors' championship.

There was also civil war at McLaren as incoming double world champion Fernando Alonso felt that he wasn't being given preference in this team that prides itself on being equitable and became increasingly agitated as he felt that rookie Lewis Hamilton – long a protege of McLaren boss Ron Dennis – was being favoured.

For Dennis, retirement had probably never seemed so attractive, with the antics at the Hungarian GP alone probably enough to encourage him to walk away. When the storm has settled, it will be remembered that his drivers went to the final race in Brazil first and second and left second and third.

Stepping up to be third best team was something that BMW Sauber seemed to do effortlessly, with Nick Heidfeld and Robert Kubica almost always the best of the rest. What has been established by Mario Theissen and the money men from Munich is a solid team that looks capable of laying down a legacy.

Renault – champions in 2005 and 2006 – dropped off the radar, with Giancarlo Fisichella becoming increasingly invisible and the emergence of rookie Heikki Kovalainen in the second half of the year the only bright spot as they struggled to become accustomed to the Bridgestone spec tyres. They escaped spying charges.

Williams on the other hand are on the way up. Their form was still maddeningly inconsistent, but they have a star in Nico Rosberg. Veteran Alex Wurz collected their only podium finish, in Canada, but that was down to canny race craft on a crazy day.

When it came to infuriating form, Red Bull Racing took the prize. The RB3 was increasingly fast, but it was too fragile and Mark Webber in particular suffered as strong point scores fell by the wayside. That he and David Coulthard were qualifiyng as high as

fifth in the final races shows how they were progressing.

Toyota continued to underperform. Their meagre points tally must be the most expensive in the sport's history and the TF107 was so tricky that even one-lap specialist Jarno Trulli struggled to slot it high on the grid. Points were hard to come by and Ralf Schumacher was dumped, perhaps not only to save budget.

It was a case of no points for Toro Rosso and then, like buses, they arrived in one hit. This was in the penultimate round, when Sebastian Vettel (who crashed out of third in the previous race) bagged fourth and Vitantonio Liuzzi took sixth, showing how a big budget has propelled the team that was once Minardi forward.

On 2007's results, Honda is going in the opposite direction, which must have been excrutiating, especially as the world knew that Rubens Barrichello and Jenson Button would have delivered had they had the car to do so. At least, a fifth place finish for Button in China saved the embarassment of being ranked behind the Super Aguri team to which they provide engines.

While there were no podiums for Honda, Super Aguri could have landed one, in Canada, but a marmot bent Anthony Davidson's front wing. However, the race yielded sixth for Takuma Sato, and he overtook Alonso's McLaren on merit.

Spyker's budget was tiny and rookie Adrian Sutil kept crashing. But he calmed down, made progress and took a point in Japan.

AUSTRALIAN GP

Kimi Raikkonen assumed Michael Schumacher's mantle at Ferrari by winning on his first race for the team, but the biggest story of all was that rookie Lewis Hamilton had shown real fighting spirit en route to third place on his Formula One debut for McLaren.

As far as Fernando Alonso was concerned, his script didn't mention being led by a debutant, his rookie team-mate Lewis Hamilton.

Change is almost always good for any sport, as it stirs up interest, and almost never more so than in Formula One. Indeed, fans of change had three reasons to be cheerful. Firstly, the most successful driver ever, Michael Schumacher, was not in the mix. Secondly, several of the leading players had changed teams. And, thirdly, there were some bright new faces to learn, most notably McLaren's Lewis Hamilton.

Kimi Raikkonen stamped his mark on qualifying to prove that the team's late-season form in 2006 had been built upon. He wound up more than 0.4s faster than the next driver, reigning world champion Fernando Alonso who had replaced him at McLaren. This was something of a surprise,

as team-mate Felipe Massa had been faster throughout winter testing. The Brazilian had been faster through much of practice too. Yet, when it counted, The Ice Man delivered.

Raikkonen kept his cool at the start of the race, too, leading into and out of Melbourne's tricky first corner. Not that Massa would have been able to challenge for the lead, though, as a gearbox problem left him 16th and he would start from the back of the 22-car grid after the team elected to make a precautionary engine change.

Alonso ought to have been second down to Turn 1, but Nick Heidfeld was starting the race with a light fuel load in his BMW Sauber and quickly demoted him to third. That wasn't the end of Alonso's embarrassment either,

as Hamilton pulled off one of the moves of the season to demote him further, taking the outside line into this tightish right-hander. Making this even more surprising was the fact that Hamilton had lost a place to Robert Kubica in the second BMW Sauber but jinked to the left and went first past the Pole and then by turning in ultra late made it by Alonso too. As one, the press corps cheered, as they like nothing better than the rattling of the establishment.

Raikkonen controlled the race from the front. He reckoned correctly that he would be making the first of his two pitstops earlier than the McLarens and was proved right when he came in on lap 19 and Hamilton pitted four laps later. Having been rattled by losing two places at the start, and especially to have been passed so boldly by his rookie team-mate, Alonso was able to save face when the young Briton – Formula One's first coloured driver – lost out when they made their second pits top. Hamilton had reason to fume after being delayed by Super Aguri's Takuma Sato on his in-lap, but his eventual third place made him the first driver to visit the podium on his debut since Jacques Villeneuve did so in 1996. It was enough to make him grin like a Cheshire Cat. Not too surprisingly, the press just wouldn't leave him alone afterwards, but Hamilton took this all in his stride.

Heidfeld showed how much progress BMW Sauber had made by racing to fourth place, while Giancarlo Fisichella's fifth place emphasised how Renault had lost ground. At least he scored, though, as new team-mate Heikki Kovalainen had a mess of a weekend. Massa deserves special mention for the manner in which he carved his way through the field to finish in sixth place, crossing the line right on Fisichella's tail.

Of the rest, Nico Rosberg equalled his best result in seventh to show that Williams had made up ground, with Ralf Schumacher the better of the Toyota drivers in taking the final point. All three of these drivers were lapped, though, as Ferrari and McLaren showed that they would be the teams to beat.

MELBOURNE ROUND 01

Date: **18 March 2007** Laps: **58** Distance: **191.110 miles/307.562km**
Weather: **Warm and bright**

RACE RESULT

Position	Driver	Team	Result	Stops	Qualifying Time	Grid
1	Kimi Räikkönen	Ferrari	1h25m28.770s	2	1m26.072s	1
2	Fernando Alonso	McLaren	1h25m36.012s	2	1m26.493s	2
3	Lewis Hamilton	McLaren	1h25m47.365s	2	1m26.755s	4
4	Nick Heidfeld	BMW Sauber	1h26m07.533s	2	1m26.756s	3
5	Giancarlo Fisichella	Renault	1h26m35.239s	2	1m27.634s	6
6	Felipe Massa	Ferrari	1h26m35.575s	1	no time	22*
7	Nico Rosberg	Williams	57 laps	2	1m26.914s	12
8	Ralf Schumacher	Toyota	57 laps	2	1m28.692s	9
9	Jarno Trulli	Toyota	57 laps	2	1m28.404s	8
10	Heikki Kovalainen	Renault	57 laps	2	1m26.964s	13
11	Rubens Barrichello	Honda	57 laps	2	1m27.679s	16
12	Takuma Sato	Super Aguri	57 laps	2	1m28.871s	10
13	Mark Webber	Red Bull	57 laps	2	1m27.934s	7
14	Vitantonio Liuzzi	Toro Rosso	57 laps	2	1m29.267s	19
15	Jenson Button	Honda	57 laps	3	1m27.264s	14
16	Anthony Davidson	Super Aguri	56 laps	2	1m26.909s	11
17	Adrian Sutil	Spyker	56 laps	4	1m29.339s	20
R	Alexander Wurz	Williams	48 laps/crash damage	1	1m27.393s	15
R	David Coulthard	Red Bull	48 laps/accident	2	1m28.579s	18
R	Robert Kubica	BMW Sauber	36 laps/gearbox	1	1m27.347s	5
R	Scott Speed	Toro Rosso	28 laps/tyre	1	1m28.305s	17
R	Christijan Albers	Spyker	10 laps/accident	0	1m31.932s	21

FASTEST LAP: RAIKKONEN, 1M25.235S, 139.173MPH/223.978KPH ON LAP 41
RACE LEADERS: RAIKKONEN, 1-17, 23-42, 45-58; HAMILTON, 19-22; ALONSO, 43-44
* STARTED FROM THE BACK OF THE GRID AFTER AN ENGINE CHANGE

TALKING POINT: HONDA GO FROM HEROES TO ZEROES

Just as some go up, others come down and this is what Honda found at Albert Park. In fact, their fall from the third place that Jenson Button had scored in the 2006 finale had already been identified in close-season testing. Sadly for the team that scored its first win in its modern incarnation in Hungary in 2006, it gained more attention for its sponsorship-free livery than for ihs on-track form. Button started 14th and Rubens Barrichello 16th. Both were lapped, with Barrichello finishing 11th and Button 15th after a drive-through. Barrichello was even more vexed as he was trapped behind Button in the first stint when running with a light fuel load.

Interesting new livery, but dreadful form summed up the state of the play for Button and Barrichello.

MALAYSIAN GP

Beaten for speed in the opening round at Melbourne, McLaren came back at Ferrari in the heat and humidity of Malaysia and made their luck by the first corner, then rode it all the way to the finish for a Fernando Alonso-Lewis Hamilton one-two.

Pole position for Ferrari – this time for Felipe Massa rather than Kimi Raikkonen – showed that they were on top in qualifying at Sepang, but their advantage had been whittled away as McLaren's Fernando Alonso was but 0.267s adrift, and this over the course of a marginally longer lap. That Massa was to pit first in the race emphasised that the gap was even less when fuel load was considered.

Raikkonen would line up third with Hamilton, who made a slight mistake on his best qualifying lap, fourth, still half a second faster than the better of the BMW Sauber drivers, Nick Heidfeld. Starting sixth

was Nico Rosberg, again emphasising how Williams, now Toyota-engined of course, were making progress.

Despite starting with the lightest fuel load of the frontrunners, Massa didn't make the best getaway and Alonso was ahead before they reached the ever-tightening first corner. But worse was to follow as Hamilton followed suit to dive inside Raikkonen for third. Making a mockery of his lack of Formula One experience, but displaying graphically his racer's instinct, Hamilton wasn't finished at that and duly kept to the outside line and ran right the way around and past Massa as the track cut

back on itself through Turn 2. McLaren were first and second, and Alonso was delighted when he looked into his mirrors and realised that his team-mate would be able to keep the Ferraris at bay while he attempted to make good his escape.

That the Ferraris weren't able to fight back, even when in close behind Hamilton in the opening stint, was revealed later to have been down to concerns over their F2007s' engine cooling efficiency in the searing temperatures. To this end, the team had chosen to fit larger cooling ducts that did the job required but hampered the aerodynamics.

A one-two for McLaren suggested that Fernando Alonso would be successful and dutifully supported all year by Lewis Hamilton...

And so it was that Alonso raced clear and Hamilton, dehydrated and without water in the final stint, did enough to hold off Raikkonen for McLaren's first one-two finish since the 2005 Brazilian GP.

Ferrari weren't able to claim the next two positions, as fourth place was taken by BMW Sauber's Heidfeld after the fuel-light Massa had tripped up when trying to repass Hamilton early in the race and fell off the track at Turn 4. Just two laps earlier, he had got ahead, but had entered Turn 4 too fast and Hamilton simply kept left and then dived back in front again on the exit.

Robert Kubica ought to have been next up, having passed Rosberg for sixth on the opening lap with another strong getaway, but he'd damaged his car's front wing in a clash with his own team-mate at Turn 1, pitted soon after because of a puncture and struggled thereafter, finishing out of the points. Rosberg should thus have finished sixth, but he lost the position after the second round of pit stops when hydraulic failure struck

And so, some considerable distance behind Massa, Giancarlo Fisichella claimed the three points with Renault team-mate Heikki Kovalainen showing an improvement in form from his troubled debut in Melbourne to finish a few seconds and two positions behind. Between them was Toyota's Jarno Trulli.

SEPANG ROUND 02

Date: **8 April 2007**   Laps: **56**   Distance: **192.887 miles/310.407km**
Weather: **Very hot and bright**

RACE RESULT

Position	Driver	Team	Result	Stops	Qualifying Time	Grid
1	Fernando Alonso	McLaren	1h32m14.930s	2	1m35.310s	2
2	Lewis Hamilton	McLaren	1h32m32.487s	2	1m36.045s	4
3	Kimi Räikkönen	Ferrari	1h32m33.269s	2	1m35.479s	3
4	Nick Heidfeld	BMW Sauber	1h32m48.707s	2	1m36.543s	5
5	Felipe Massa	Ferrari	1h32m51.635s	2	1m35.043s	1
6	Giancarlo Fisichella	Renault	1h33m20.568s	2	1m35.706s	12
7	Jarno Trulli	Toyota	1h33m25.062s	2	1m36.902s	8
8	Heikki Kovalainen	Renault	1h33m26.945s	2	1m35.630s	11
9	Alexander Wurz	Williams	1h33m44.854s	2	1m37.326s	20
10	Mark Webber	Red Bull	1h33m48.486s	2	1m37.345s	10
11	Rubens Barrichello	Honda	55 laps	2	1m36.827s	19
12	Jenson Button	Honda	55 laps	2	1m36.088s	15
13	Takuma Sato	Super Aguri	55 laps	2	1m35.945s	14
14	Scott Speed	Toro Rosso	55 laps	2	1m36.578s	17
15	Ralf Schumacher	Toyota	55 laps	2	1m37.078s	9
16	Anthony Davidson	Super Aguri	55 laps	2	1m36.816s	18
17	Vitantonio Liuzzi	Toro Rosso	55 laps	3	1m36.145s	16
18	Robert Kubica	BMW Sauber	55 laps	2	1m36.896s	7
R	Nico Rosberg	Williams	42 laps/water leak	2	1m36.829s	6
R	David Coulthard	Red Bull	36 laps/steering	1	1m35.766s	13
R	Christijan Albers	Spyker	7 laps/gearbox	0	1m38.279s	21
R	Adrian Sutil	Spyker	0 laps/accident	0	1m38.415s	22

FASTEST LAP: HAMILTON, 1M36.701S, 128.224MPH/206.357KPH ON LAP 22
RACE LEADERS: ALONSO, 1-18, 22-40, 42-56; HAMILTON, 19-20; HEIDFELD, 21; RAIKKONEN, 41

TALKING POINT: DEFINING WHAT IS A CUSTOMER CAR

You couldn't blame Spyker striking out at two teams it felt was standing between it and financially crucial points by running cars that were strikingly similar to those of other teams. Indeed, Spyker team principal Colin Kolles was busy for a second race trying to prove that the Super Aguri SA07 was all but the Honda RA106 and the Toro Rosso STR2 simply the Red Bull RB3 with a different engine. If this was the case, they would be in breach of the Concorde Agreement. Strengthening his claim, he'd received a blueprint appearing to show that the STR2 and RB3 were the same. However, the FIA stewards in Malaysia threw out his protest.

The similarity between Toro Rosso and the cars from sister team Red Bull was more than coincidental.

BAHRAIN GP

First Ferrari, then McLaren and now Ferrari again as the pendulum swung again. Yet, showing that Ferrari is now a true two-driver team, it was Felipe Massa rather than Kimi Raikkonen who took the honours, with young Hamilton splitting the duo.

Felipe Massa made it three different winners in the first three grands prix on a day when the numbers two at Ferrari and McLaren came good.

Pole position for the second race in succession went to Felipe Massa and he was joined for the first time on the front row by Lewis Hamilton, meaning that both of the top teams had to acknowledge that their number twos were outgunning their supposed lead drivers. They would line up on the second row, with the BMW Saubers of Nick Heidfeld and Robert Kubica again the best of the rest.

This time, no doubt giving his all to avoid his slip-ups at the Malaysian GP, Massa made a clean start, resisting the inevitable first corner attack from Hamilton, and staying in front except for during his two pit stops for the remaining 55 laps.

Hamilton tucked into second place, with Raikkonen again being caught out at the start as Alonso went past him into third. This wasn't the only time in the race that the Finn seemed to be asleep as he also made a mess of his restart after running in the wake of the safety car, failing to stick to the tail of the car ahead on the safety car's in-lap and thus losing ground both for himself and for the cars bunched behind. The safety car had been called out on lap 2 as Jenson Button and Scott Speed had collided at Turn 4 after Button had been hit by Adrian Sutil's Stryker and Speed's Toro Rosso was left stranded on the circuit.

While Massa's drive was faultless and did

a considerable amount for re-establishing his name after his slapdash race in Malaysia, and Hamilton's drive to his third straight podium was remarkable, much of the talk in the paddock post-race was centred on Nick Heidfeld's overtaking manoeuvre on Alonso. It came on lap 31 and took place at Turn 4, with the German driver carrying more momentum after the Spaniard was compromised on his exit from the Turn 1/2 complex as he defended his position from the pressing BMW Sauber. Impressively, Heidfeld simply drove around the outside, not backing off an iota as they all but touched wheels. He was then able to keep Alonso behind thereafter.

Heidfeld's team-mate Robert Kubica came home sixth, slowed by a fuel flap that remained open. Such was the advantage of these top three teams that the seventh-placed driver, Jarno Trulli, was 35s further back as he fought to keep his Toyota ahead of Giancarlo Fisichella's Renault.

Honda had another stinker, with Button out as mentioned on lap 1, and Rubens Barrichello finishing a lapped 13th. Small wonder, then, that the Japanese manufacturer had already commissioned a B-specification car to be ready later in the campaign.

David Coulthard deserves mention. The Red Bull driver didn't make it to the finish, but he'd displayed a fighter's heart as he worked his way forward after starting last but one following gearbox problems in qualifying. He climbed as high as seventh, even passing his team-mate Mark Webber before a driveshaft failed. Completing Red Bull's set of retirements, Webber was also out before the end as a gearbox failure cost him a possible point or two. At least, the team said, there had been improved speed before the failures, and the drivers were happy to work with a faster but fragile car than a slow but steady one.

Amazingly, after three races, Alonso, Hamilton and Raikkonen were equal on points for the lead of the world championship.

BAHRAIN ROUND 03
Date: **15 April 2007** Laps: **57** Distance: **191.530 miles/308.238km**
Weather: **Very hot and bright**

RACE RESULT

Position	Driver	Team	Result	Stops	Qualifying Time	Grid
1	Felipe Massa	Ferrari	1h33m27.515s	2	1m32.652s	1
2	Lewis Hamilton	McLaren	1h33m29.875s	2	1m32.935s	2
3	Kimi Räikkönen	Ferrari	1h33m38.354s	2	1m33.131s	3
4	Nick Heidfeld	BMW Sauber	1h33m41.346s	2	1m33.404s	5
5	Fernando Alonso	McLaren	1h33m41.941s	2	1m33.192s	4
6	Robert Kubica	BMW Sauber	1h34m13.044s	2	1m33.710s	6
7	Jarno Trulli	Toyota	1h34m48.886s	2	1m34.154s	9
8	Giancarlo Fisichella	Renault	1h34m49.216s	2	1m34.056s	7
9	Heikki Kovalainen	Renault	1h34m56.926s	2	1m32.935s	12
10	Nico Rosberg	Williams	1h34m57.431s	2	1m34.399s	10
11	Alexander Wurz	Williams	56 laps	2	1m32.915s	11
12	Ralf Schumacher	Toyota	56 laps	2	1m33.294s	14
13	Rubens Barrichello	Honda	56 laps	2	1m33.624s	15
14	Christijan Albers	Spyker	55 laps	2	1m35.533s	22
15	Adrian Sutil	Spyker	53 laps	3	1m35.280s	20
16	Anthony Davidson	Super Aguri	51 laps/engine	2	1m33.082s	13
R	Mark Webber	Red Bull	41 laps/gearbox	2	1m34.106s	8
R	David Coulthard	Red Bull	36 laps/driveshaft	2	1m35.341s	21
R	Takuma Sato	Super Aguri	34 laps/engine	1	1m33.984s	17
R	Vitantonio Liuzzi	Toro Rosso	26 laps/hydraulics	2	1m34.024s	18
R	Scott Speed	Toro Rosso	0 laps/collision	0	1m34.333s	19
R	Jenson Button	Honda	0 laps/collision	0	1m33.731s	16

FASTEST LAP: MASSA, 1M34.067S, 128.720MPH/207.155KPH ON LAP 42
RACE LEADERS: MASSA, 1-21, 24-40, 45-56; RAIKKONEN, 22-23; HAMILTON, 41-44

TALKING POINT: NICK HEIDFELD KEEPS PRODUCING THE GOODS

With Ferrari and McLaren the two best teams at the start of 2007, it was with huge respect that insiders viewed Nick Heidfeld's first three finishes of fourth, fourth and fourth. Especially so, it must be said, as he beat world champion Fernando Alonso in Bahrain by outwitting him out on the track. So, finally, the driver who had seemed the equal of Juan Pablo Montoya when they fought over the Formula 3000 title in 1998 had the tools of the job and was making the most of them. No wonder, then, that his name was being linked to taking over from Ralf Schumacher at Toyota for 2008, although this was seen simply as a gambit to boost his salary.

John Watson shaved off his beard after his first win. People wandered if Heidfeld would be following suit.

SPANISH GP

The number twos proved the number ones for the second race running as Felipe Massa and Kimi Raikkonen outshone their team leaders again. Fernando Alonso was desperate to give the fans a home win, but it all went wrong at the first corner.

Fernando Alonso was not only desperate to win at home but also to keep Hamilton behind him and this mistake was the result of the pressure.

Traditionally, Ferrari has a number one driver and his back-up, as witnessed during Michael Schumacher's reign. McLaren tends to let its drivers have their head. But there is no doubting that both Kimi Raikkonen and reigning world champion Fernando Alonso would have expected to be the top dogs at Ferrari and McLaren respectively in 2007. On the evidence of what occured at the Circuit de Catalunya, they were going to have to push harder to assume control.

Put simply, Raikkonen appeared still to be struggling to get the most out of Bridgestone tyres, particularly in qualifying, after transferring from McLaren that had, of course, been Michelin-shod in 2006. Alonso, on the other hand, was making progress after a lacklustre time when he was outshone by team-mate Lewis Hamilton in Bahrain, but tried too hard at the first corner on the opening lap and found himself pushed wide onto the gravel by pole-starter Felipe Massa. This lost him time and, more importantly, position. The matter was compounded in that not only did he fall behind Raikkonen, but fast-starting Hamilton passed the pair to slot into second place. As Alonso had started with a light fuel load, this was a double disaster, leaving him bottled up when he should have been flying.

Alonso did get up to third, but only after Raikkonen parked his Ferrari with an electrical problem on lap 9. The Finn then promptly left the circuit, something that Ferrari's guest visitor Michael Schumacher never did when he was racing as he certainly never ducked out of any form of debrief.

Massa ran untroubled at the front, with Hamilton easily clear of Alonso. And this is how they stayed to flagfall, with Alonso's gamble of running his harder set of tyres in the middle stint not bringing him out ahead of Hamilton for the run to the chequered flag.

Raikkonen's departure promoted Robert Kubica by one position. The Pole's cause was aided further when his BMW Sauber team-mate Nick Heidfeld was flagged away from his first pitstop before one of his wheels was fully attached, triggering a slow lap and a race ruined. This elevated David Coulthard to fifth and he didn't put a foot wrong as he gave Red Bull its first points of the year. An attack from Renault's Heikki Kovalainen kept him on his toes until the pressure was relieved when the Finn had a fuel rig problem that necessitated him making an extra stop. Then a loss of third gear in the closing laps caused concern, forcing David to drive in fourth gear and above, but he did just enough to hold off Nico Rosberg's Williams, later saying that there was better to come.

The thorny issue of customer cars played out at Barcelona in a way that its critics didn't expect when Super Aguri - whose car bore a clear resemblance to the 2006 Honda - finished higher than Honda. Indeed, not only was this the case, but Takuma Sato raced to the team's first world championship points, having advanced from 13th on the grid. The point that he realised that he'd done enough was when he was just in front of Giancarlo Fisichella's Renault when it emerged from its second pit stop. So, a team that had been at the back in its maiden season was able to head home the team that had been top of the pile in 2006, which is significant progress in anyone's book.

CATALUNYA ROUND 04

Date: **13 May 2007** Laps: **65** Distance: **183.170 miles/294.784km**
Weather: **Hot and bright**

RACE RESULT

Position	Driver	Team	Result	Stops	Qualifying Time	Grid
1	Felipe Massa	Ferrari	1h31m36.230s	2	1m21.421s	1
2	Lewis Hamilton	McLaren	1h31m43.020s	2	1m21.785s	4
3	Fernando Alonso	McLaren	1h31m53.686s	2	1m21.451s	2
4	Robert Kubica	BMW Sauber	1h32m07.845s	2	1m22.253s	5
5	David Coulthard	Red Bull	1h32m34.561s	2	1m22.749s	9
6	Nico Rosberg	Williams	1h32m35.768s	2	1m21.968s	11
7	Heikki Kovalainen	Renault	1h32m38.358s	3	1m22.568s	6
8	Takuma Sato	Super Aguri	64 laps	2	1m22.115s	13
9	Giancarlo Fisichella	Renault	64 laps	2	1m22.881s	10
10	Rubens Barrichello	Honda	64 laps	2	1m22.097s	12
11	Anthony Davidson	Super Aguri	64 laps	2	no time	15
12	Jenson Button	Honda	64 laps	3	1m22.120s	14
13	Adrian Sutil	Spyker	63 laps	2	1m23.811s	20
14	Christijan Albers	Spyker	63 laps	3	1m23.990s	21
R	Nick Heidfeld	BMW Sauber	46 laps/gearbox	2	1m22.389s	7
R	Ralf Schumacher	Toyota	44 laps/loose nose	2	1m22.666s	17
R	Vitantonio Liuzzi	Toro Rosso	19 laps/hydraulics	0	no time	16
R	Scott Speed	Toro Rosso	9 laps/tyre	0	no time	22
R	Kimi Räikkönen	Ferrari	9 laps/electrics	0	1m21.723s	3
R	Jarno Trulli	Toyota	8 laps/fuel line	0	1m22.324s	6*
R	Mark Webber	Red Bull	7 laps/hydraulics	0	1m23.398s	19
R	Alexander Wurz	Williams	1 lap/crash damage	0	1m22.769s	18

FASTEST LAP: MASSA, 1M22.680S, 122.700MPH/197.467KPH ON LAP 14
RACE LEADERS: MASSA, 1-19, 25-42, 48-65; HAMILTON, 20-22, 43-47; HEIDFELD, 23-24
* STARTED FROM THE PITLANE

TALKING POINT: SPAIN TO HOST TWO GRANDS PRIX IN 2008

Formula One supremo Bernie Ecclestone sure knows how to play parties off against each other, so his choice of the week of the Spanish GP to announce neighbouring Valencia would be on the 2008 calendar with a grand prix of its was typical. By the end of the weekend, though, Ecclestone and the Barcelona venue's management had completed their deal for the continuation of the Spanish GP at the Circuit de Catalunya until 2016. This new grand prix, sparked by the Alonso-led surge of popularity for Formula One in Spain is to be held on a circuit around Valencia's port area that had been tidied up for hosting the America's Cup yacht races.

Bernie Ecclestone rewarded Spain's blossoming interest in Formula One with a second grand prix.

MONACO GP

McLaren has always been seen as a team that lets its drivers race rather than operating a driver preference, but the focus after their runaway one-two in Monaco was on whether Hamilton had been made to play second fiddle to Alonso.

It's a funny old world in Formula One. The team's 14th win in the Principality since Ron Dennis took over McLaren in 1980 ought to have triggered wild celebration, especially as the team they trailed at the start of the season, Ferrari, was a minute behind when the chequered flag fell. Yet, here was the team going about its post-race celebrations in a somewhat muted way, with Lewis Hamilton's less than cheery face on the podium suggesting that all wasn't quite well in the camp.

 The British rookie had finished a handful of seconds behind his team-mate Fernando Alonso, but he wasn't happy and made it plain

in the post-podium press conference that he felt that he'd been held back by the team, possibly costing him his first win (see box-out). Certainly, Alonso had been sent out for his final qualifying run with less fuel on board and duly took pole position, from which he led into the first corner at the start of the race. However, all teams employ this tactic so that they don't have both of their drivers coming in for their first pit stop on the same lap. What annoyed Hamilton, though – apart from the fact that his final qualifying run was delayed through Casino Square by Mark Webber's Red Bull and this probably cost him the pole that is so vital on the narrow Monaco street circuit

– was that he had been told to bring his car in for its pit stops earlier than planned. This might have cost him his chance to go for gold. He might have been right, and he was also fuelled for longer than Alonso, but it was an order from team supremo Ron Dennis during this second stint for his drivers to back off to save their brakes and that certainly removed the likelihood of the tyro clashing with the the double world champion. Understandably, McLaren was delighted to come away with maximum points as it pulls clear of arch-rivals Ferrari, Hamilton less so.

Following Hamilton's post-race comments suggesting that the number on the nose of his

He who reaches the first corner ahead at Monaco tends to win. This is Fernando Alonso achieving just that for McLaren.

car, two, showed his place in the team, Dennis faced down the press and explained that what they had been watching was a win through team strategy rather than team orders.

What of the rest? Well, Felipe Massa started third and finished third, albeit more than a minute adrift of Hamilton, who was 'cruising' don't forget. The finger was pointed at the F2007's long-wheelbase format for its less than sparkling form around the tightly twisting circuit. Team-mate Kimi Raikkonen had had to start 16th after failing to set a time in the second qualifying session, but came through to snatch the final point.

Renault displayed improved form and Giancarlo Fisichella, although lapped, was delighted to put the one-stopping BMW Saubers behind him, with Robert Kubica finishing ahead of Nick Heidfeld.

Alexander Wurz scored his first points since 2005 by using a heavy starting fuel load to jump the Hondas, but special mention must be made of Scott Speed who came home ninth for Toro Rosso, having gained four places at Ste Devote on lap one. Team-mate Vitantonio Liuzzi wasn't so fortunate, having been clouted up the rear at that same opening corner by David Coulthard whose Red Bull never handled well after that. His team-mate Mark Webber, who started sixth, lost points when his car lost third gear.

MONACO ROUND 05

Date: **27 May 2007** Laps: **78** Distance: **161.880 miles/260.520km**
Weather: **Warm and bright**

RACE RESULT

Position	Driver	Team	Result	Stops	Qualifying Time	Grid
1	Fernando Alonso	McLaren	1h40m29.329s	2	1m15.726s	1
2	Lewis Hamilton	McLaren	1h40m33.424s	2	1m15.905s	2
3	Felipe Massa	Ferrari	1h41m38.443s	2	1m15.967s	3
4	Giancarlo Fisichella	Renault	77 laps	2	1m16.285s	4
5	Robert Kubica	BMW Sauber	77 laps	1	1m16.955s	8
6	Nick Heidfeld	BMW Sauber	77 laps	1	1m16.832s	7
7	Alexander Wurz	Williams	77 laps	1	1m16.662s	11
8	Kimi Räikkönen	Ferrari	77 laps	1	No time	16
9	Scott Speed	Toro Rosso	77 laps	1	1m18.390s	18
10	Rubens Barrichello	Honda	77 laps	2	1m17.498s	9
11	Jenson Button	Honda	77 laps	2	1m17.939s	10
12	Nico Rosberg	Williams	77 laps	2	1m16.439s	5
13	Heikki Kovalainen	Renault	76 laps	1	1m17.125s	15
14	David Coulthard	Red Bull	76 laps	1	1m16.319s	13*
15	Jarno Trulli	Toyota	76 laps	1	1m16.988s	14
16	Ralf Schumacher	Toyota	76 laps	1	1m18.539s	20
17	Takuma Sato	Super Aguri	76 laps	2	1m18.554s	21
18	Anthony Davidson	Super Aguri	76 laps	2	1m18.250s	17
19	Christijan Albers	Spyker	70 laps/driveshaft	2	No time	22
R	Adrian Sutil	Spyker	53 laps/spun off	1	1m18.418s	19
R	Mark Webber	Red Bull	17 laps/gearbox	0	1m16.784s	6
R	Vitantonio Liuzzi	Toro Rosso	1 lap/spun off	0	1m16.703s	12

FASTEST LAP: FERNANDO ALONSO, 1M15.284S, 99.242MPH/159.715KPH ON LAP 44
RACE LEADERS: ALONSO, 1-25, 29-50, 53-78; HAMILTON, 26-28, 51-52
* INCLUDING TWO-PLACE GRID PENALTY

TALKING POINT: MEDIA CLAIMS THAT McLAREN USED TEAM ORDERS

Lewis Hamilton wasn't smiling much after finishing second. If Lewis wasn't happy, though, that was nothing compared to the British press who had been hoping for its new darling's first win. Their high dudgeon led to the sport's governing body investigating the matter. After checking McLaren's radio messages, the FIA declared that McLaren had not transgressed the rule that no team orders may be employed. Indeed, it wasn't as though McLaren had ordered the driver in front to slow to let the one behind go past to win, as Ferrari asked Rubens Barrichello to do at the 2002 Austrian GP, triggering a massed protest and a rewriting of the rules.

Ron Dennis faced up to the media to explain why the team was having to take a cautious approach.

CANADIAN GP

When headlines heralded Lewis Hamilton's maiden win, they said that it was the start of something big. They weren't wrong in that, especially as his victory was hard fought, repelling the attacks of his world champion team-mate Alonso.

Rookies almost never win races. Jacques Villeneuve did, Juan Pablo Montoya did, but none since until Lewis Hamilton rolled into Montreal. He arrived with a third place in the opening round followed by four second places, but a problem in out-qualifying his McLaren team-mate Fernando Alonso – the reigning world champion, no less – left the 22-year-old anxious to be allowed by the team to give it his best shot with a lightish fuel load. This they acceded to and Lewis did the rest, taking pole by 0.456s over Alonso.

Getting to the first corner first is critical at the Circuit Gilles Villeneuve, and Alonso pressed the slow-starting Hamilton, but Alonso was in danger of dropping to third as Nick Heidfeld made yet another excellent start. In defending his position, Alonso ran across the grass and fell behind Heidfeld.

Felipe Massa ran side-by-side with his Ferrari team-mate on the run to the first corner, with Kimi Raikkonen being forced wide when Alonso rejoined in front of Massa, losing a place to Williams' Nico Rosberg.

As Hamilton edged clear of Heidfeld, Alonso continued to make a mess of Turn 1, running wide twice more, with the second of these excursions letting Massa by.

Heidfeld was the first to pit. Hamilton hadn't been due to come in, but McLaren brought his first scheduled stop forward by as many as four laps so that he wouldn't be caught out if a safety car had to be deployed. This was a masterstroke, as Adrian Sutil hit the wall at Turn 4 that very lap. Those due to stay out longer, such as Alonso and Rosberg, were now unable to pit because the pit entry was closed until everyone had lined up in order behind the safety car, with

lapped cars allowed to unlap themselves. Yet, with fuel running low, they had to come in, and so both collected a stop-go penalty.

For those who could eke out their fuel load, there was a scramble when the pit lane reopened, with Hamilton and Heidfeld returning to the front as Massa pitted and fell down the order as he found the pit exit lights to be on red. Massa and Giancarlo Fisichella chose to leave, both driving past

Robert Kubica's BMW Sauber. It was to prove their undoing, as both were disqualified.

Hamilton's composure is such that he wasn't expected to trip up when the safety car finally came in, and it was he rather than Heidfeld who had the hammer down. He got the chance to show his restart skills again soon afterwards as the safety car was almost immediately called for again as Kubica had been launched into a fearsome

The safety car led much of the race, but Hamilton was always able to keep Heidfeld behind him.

barrell-rolling accident that only a handful of years ago would have killed him (see feature on page 56).

Hamilton was on it again after the third restart, following Christijan Albers crashing his Spyker and scattering debris across the track at Turn 8, and his patience was tested further when the safety car came out yet again so Vitantonio Liuzzi's crashed Toro Rosso could be removed. Yet he remained in control all the way to the finish, keeping his head while all around lost theirs.

Heidfeld had been demoted by Mark Webber until he made his a late pit stop and fell down the order, but the German was able to finish second, equalling his best result.

That third place went to a driver who started 19th, Alex Wurz, is down to an inspired one-stop strategy from Williams. Almost as inspired was Super Aguri's decision to bring Takuma Sato in twice during the third safety car period to fit then discard the supersoft rubber that didn't suit it before racing past Ralf Schumacher then Alonso with three laps to go. It was a sight that few could believe, as the reigning world champion struggled on his supersofts. Sato's team-mate Anthony Davidson might even have finished third, but he hit a marmot and the resultant pitstops to clear it out and then replace the front wing dropped him to 11th.

MONTREAL ROUND 06

Date: **10 June 2007** Laps: **70** Distance: **189.686 miles/305.270km**
Weather: **Warm and bright**

RACE RESULT

Position	Driver	Team	Result	Stops	Qualifying Time	Grid
1	Lewis Hamilton	McLaren	1h44m11.292s	2	1m15.707s	1
2	Nick Heidfeld	BMW Sauber	1h44m15.635s	2	1m16.266s	3
3	Alexander Wurz	Williams	1h44m16.617s	1	1m18.089s	19
4	Heikki Kovalainen	Renault	1h44m18.021s	2	1m17.806s	22*
5	Kimi Räikkönen	Ferrari	1h44m24.299s	2	1m16.411s	4
6	Takuma Sato	Super Aguri	1h44m27.990s	3	1m16.743s	11
7	Fernando Alonso	McLaren	1h44m33.228s	3	1m16.163s	2
8	Ralf Schumacher	Toyota	1h44m34.180s	2	1m17.634s	18
9	Mark Webber	Red Bull	1h44m34.252s	2	1m16.913s	6
10	Nico Rosberg	Williams	1h44m35.276s	2	1m16.919s	7
11	Anthony Davidson	Super Aguri	1h44m35.610s	3	1m17.452s	17
12	Rubens Barrichello	Honda	1h44m41.731s	3	1m17.116s	13
R	Jarno Trulli	Toyota	58 laps/spun off	4	1m17.747s	10
R	Vitantonio Liuzzi	Toro Rosso	54 laps/spun off	3	1m16.760s	12
D	Felipe Massa	Ferrari	51 laps/pit infringement	1	1m16.570s	5
D	Giancarlo Fisichella	Renault	51 laps/pit infringement	2	1m17.229s	9
R	Christijan Albers	Spyker	47 laps/spun off	1	1m19.196s	21
R	David Coulthard	Red Bull	36 laps/gearbox	3	1m17.304s	14
R	Robert Kubica	BMW Sauber	26 laps/spun off	1	1m16.993s	8
R	Adrian Sutil	Spyker	21 laps/spun off	0	1m18.536s	20
R	Scott Speed	Toro Rosso	8 laps/collision	0	1m17.571s	16
R	Jenson Button	Honda	0 laps/transmission	0	1m17.541s	15

FASTEST LAP: ALONSO 1M16.367S (127.786MPH/205.652KPH) ON LAP 46
RACE LEADERS: HAMILTON 1-21, 25-70, MASSA 22-24
* 10-PLACE ENGINE-CHANGE GRID PENALTY

TALKING POINT: HAMILTON SCORES THE FIRST OF MANY

The headlines said it all: this could be the start of something big for Lewis Hamilton. And for Formula One too as he continued to introduce new fans to the sport and entice old ones back who had turned away when Michael Schumacher had made it all too inevitable. Chiefly, though, people the world over, and certainly the media, were excited by the way Lewis went about his business, with a supersmooth style but with an undercurrent of steel when it was needed. Good looking, modest, black and young, he was being heralded as the new face of Formula One and sponsors were already beating a path to his door, sure that there were more wins on the way.

It says it all on the side of Lewis's cap as he sprays the Champagne: 1st. Yes, the first of many.

UNITED STATES GP

Two McLarens jousting side-by-side down the main straight at Indianapolis was one of the key moments of 2007, for it showed that reigning World Champion Fernando Alonso had a real battle on his hands in team-mate Lewis Hamilton.

Nick Heidfeld takes to the grass, David Coulthard is in a spin and Jenson Button heads down the escape road at Turn 1.

The organisers of the United States GP didn't know it at the time, but this was to be the Indianapolis Motor Speedway's last grand prix for the forseeable future. That being the case, they were treated to a classic. Yes, it was McLaren, a gap, then Ferrari, then another gap and then the rest, but tyro Lewis Hamilton and double World Champion Fernando Alonso provided the entertainment.

Hamilton had grabbed pole, for the second race in a row, and he wanted to win, for the second race in a row. Indeed, having whetted his appetite with his maiden win just a week earlier in Montreal, he was hungry for more.

Leading away from pole and staying ahead into the first corner was imperative. Certainly, Alonso would try to get past and

try he did, but Hamilton had just enough of a lead to claim the line for the tightish right-left sequence at the end of the straight. Alonso slotted in behind and sat there, keeping Hamilton under pressure but aware that he ought to have enough fuel on board to run an opening stint a lap longer than his rookie team-mate's. With Ferrari's Felipe Massa unable to match his pace in third, Alonso was safe to relax. Kimi Raikkonen ought to have been next up, but he stumbled at the start and was passed immediately by Nick Heidfeld's BMW Sauber and Heikki Kovalainen's Renault.

There was trouble further down the field as Ralf Schumacher locked up his Toyota and slid into David Coulthard's Red Bull, with Rubens Barrichello having to swerve to avoid

hitting the Toyota and damaging his Honda against two other cars, including team-mate Jenson Button's which struggled on in damaged form for the rest of the race.

To Alonso's horror, he discovered that his tyres were graining as he ran behind Hamilton, whether in his slipstream or out of it. He was 4s down when Hamilton made his first planned pit stop and thus realised that his move for the lead would have to wait until he could see what he might manage on his second set of tyres. Once on these, a lap later, Alonso found himself still 4s down, but he gradually closed in on the race leader.

Alonso made a bid to pass Hamilton into Turn 1 on lap 38 after his team-mate lost momentum behind Vitantonio Liuzzi's Toro Rosso at Turn 11, but this 200mph tussle didn't change the order and he gesticulated at the McLaren pit wall personnel next time past, letting them know that he felt he was the faster of the duo, but sadly the one stuck in second. So, Alonso's fate was to finish second and see Hamilton's points advantage extend to 10. Still, Alonso said, at least he achieved a podium position at Indianapolis for the first time. McLaren's lead over Ferrari was extended to 35 points.

Massa joined them on the podium, with Raikkonen having worked his way back up to fourth place. Fifth ought to have gone to Heidfeld, but his car suffered hydraulic failure and so Kovalainen filled the position, with Toyota's Jarno Trulli claiming sixth ahead of Red Bull's Mark Webber.

Following his 75g accident in the Canadian GP, Robert Kubica had to attend a medical check at Indianapolis. And this he duly failed, clearing the way for BMW Sauber's test driver Sebastian Vettel to make his debut. He qualified seventh, made a slip up on the opening lap, locking up his brakes into Turn 1 and having to go straight on to avoid Kovalainen, losing four places in the process, but made amends by working his way back to eighth by race's end, thus becoming the first teenager ever to score a point, at 19 years and 349 days, beating a record set by Bruce McLaren in 1958.

INDIANAPOLIS ROUND 07
Date: **17 June 2007** Laps: **73** Distance: **190.150 miles/306.016km**
Weather: **Warm and bright**

RACE RESULT

Position	Driver	Team	Result	Stops	Qualifying Time	Grid
1	Lewis Hamilton	McLaren	1h31m09.965s	2	1m12.331s	1
2	Fernando Alonso	McLaren	1h31m11.483s	2	1m12.500s	2
3	Felipe Massa	Ferrari	1h31m22.807s	2	1m12.703s	3
4	Kimi Räikkönen	Ferrari	1h31m25.387s	2	1m12.839s	4
5	Heikki Kovalainen	Renault	1h31m51.367s	2	1m13.308s	6
6	Jarno Trulli	Toyota	1h32m16.668s	2	1m13.789s	8
7	Mark Webber	Red Bull	1h32m17.296s	2	1m13.871s	9
8	Sebastian Vettel	BMW Sauber	1h32m17.748s	2	1m13.513s	7
9	Giancarlo Fisichella	Renault	72 laps	1	1m13.953s	10
10	Alexander Wurz	Williams	72 laps	1	1m13.441s	17
11	Anthony Davidson	Super Aguri	72 laps	2	1m13.259s	16
12	Jenson Button	Honda	72 laps	1	1m13.201s	15
13	Scott Speed	Toro Rosso	71 laps	1	1m13.712s	20
14	Adrian Sutil	Spyker	71 laps	2	1m14.122s	21
15	Christijan Albers	Spyker	70 laps	1	1m14.597s	22
16	Nico Rosberg	Williams	68 laps/oil leak	1	1m13.060s	14
17	Vitantonio Liuzzi	Toro Rosso	68 laps/water leak	1	1m13.484s	19
R	Nick Heidfeld	BMW Sauber	55 laps/hydraulics	2	1m12.847s	5
R	Takuma Sato	Super Aguri	13 laps/spin	0	1m13.477s	18
R	David Coulthard	Red Bull	0 laps/accident damage	0	1m12.873s	11
R	Rubens Barrichello	Honda	0 laps/accident damage	0	1m12.998s	13
R	Ralf Schumacher	Toyota	0 laps/accident	0	1m12.920s	12

FASTEST LAP: RAIKKONEN, 1M13.117S ((128.249MPH/206.397KPH) ON LAP 49
RACE LEADERS: HAMILTON 1-20, 27-50, 52-73, ALONSO 21, KOVALAINEN 22-26, MASSA 51

TALKING POINT: RAIKKONEN COMES UNDER PRESSURE AT FERRARI

Acknowledged as one of the quickest of the quick, and a winner first time out with Ferrari in Melbourne, Kimi Raikkonen appeared to have made the right decision by switching from McLaren to Ferrari for 2007. However, this script didn't include the Finn being outdriven by his team-mate Felipe Massa. At times, though, Kimi looked out of touch, his form in Bahrain when Massa won was less than impressive. At least he finished on the podium that time, but a failure to achieve third or higher over the next four rounds meant that the knives were out and Williams racer Nico Rosberg was even said to be being lined up should no improvements come.

Raikkonen claimed the pressure wasn't getting to him, but Ferrari were less than happy with his form.

FRENCH GP

Kimi Raikkonen's form and motivation had been questioned, but this was his response, a victory that not only earned him 10 points but also put one over his Ferrari team-mate Felipe Massa. Lewis Hamilton fluffed his start but finished third.

A win is worth 10 points, but to Kimi Raikkonen, this win was worth far more than that, as it brought him back into the frame just as it was looking as though he was moving out of the picture.

The portends hadn't been good after qualifying, as there was his bete noire, team-mate Felipe Massa on pole and filling the front row with him was Lewis Hamilton, with Kimi back in third after a mistake on his quickest lap. Hamilton too was left to rue a slip-up that might have denied him pole. At least the other McLaren driver, Fernando Alonso, would be starting from back in 10th place after gearbox trouble hit him early in the final qualifying session.

The tide turned for the Finn at the very start of the race when Hamilton struggled for traction as he tried to accelerate away from the dirty side of the grid. In a flash, it was a Ferrari one-two, making team supremo Jean Todt smile for the first time in three races.

Hamilton tucked into third place, followed by Robert Kubica, Giancarlo Fisichella and Nick Heidfeld, with Alonso up two places to eighth as Jarno Trulli had tried to dive past Heikki Kovalainen's Renault into the Adelaide hairpin. It didn't work and the Toyota driver's race was run. A lap later, Alonso passed Nico Rosberg to go seventh, but here he would stay for the remainder of the race, although it certainly wasn't for the want of trying as he battled with both Heidfeld and Fisichella. Late in the race, he also had to pass the one-stopping Jenson Button.

Raikkonen's first lap demotion of Hamilton was doubly important, as it soon became clear that Hamilton couldn't match the Ferraris for pace and would have been holding Raikkonen up through the first stint had he held onto his starting position. Massa, then, would have escaped. However, by getting into second, Raikkonen was able to stay with the Brazilian right up to their pit stops. Massa was first in, on lap 19, then Raikkonen three laps later. But it was Massa who was still in front when Raikkonen rejoined, albeit with Raikkonen now just 2s behind.

Massa also came in for his second stop three laps earlier than Raikkonen, but this time their order was reversed, with Raikkonen taking a lead he wasn't to lose and Massa left to complain about being blocked by traffic

Back in the saddle after his massive accident in the Canadian GP, Robert Kubica was superb as he raced to fourth place for BMW Sauber.

midway through the stint. The margin of victory was just over 2s, but it was enough to bring a rare smile to Raikkonen's face. He was back on track and he knew it.

Hamilton simply wasn't able to live with the pace of the Ferraris and so the McLaren team decided to try another tactic and short-fuelled him at his second stop so that if his obligatory run on the soft tyre proved problematic, he'd come in and fit the medium tyre again for his final stint. He rejoined right behind Kubica after this second stop and showed what balls he has by immediately outbraking the Pole into the hairpin so that he wouldn't lose a second of time. Even though he was not in contention to tackle the Ferraris. It was a move reminiscent of the take-no-prisoners Michael Schumacher.

That was possibly the best move of the race, but the worst was that produced by Christijan Albers when he decided to leave his pit stop early, with the fuel hose still attached to his Spyker.

It was all doom and gloom for the organisers of the French GP following their race, as it was made clear that this would be the final time that Formula One would be visiting, even though its contract ran until 2011. Less than a month later, after Bernie Ecclestone met French president Francois Fillon, the race was back on for 2008 and probably 2009 as well.

MAGNY-COURS ROUND 08

Date: **1 July 2007** Laps: **70** Distance: **191.870 miles/308.785km**
Weather: **Warm but overcast**

RACE RESULT

Position	Driver	Team	Result	Stops	Qualifying Time	Grid
1	Kimi Räikkönen	Ferrari	1h30m54.200s	2	1m15.257s	3
2	Felipe Massa	Ferrari	1h30m56.614s	2	1m15.034s	1
3	Lewis Hamilton	McLaren	1h31m26.353s	3	1m15.104s	2
4	Robert Kubica	BMW Sauber	1h31m35.927s	2	1m15.493s	4
5	Nick Heidfeld	BMW Sauber	1h31m43.001s	2	1m15.900s	7
6	Giancarlo Fisichella	Renault	1h31m46.410s	2	1m15.674s	5
7	Fernando Alonso	McLaren	1h31m50.716s	2	no time	10
8	Jenson Button	Honda	1h31m53.085s	2	1m15.584s	12
9	Nico Rosberg	Williams	1h32m02.705s	2	1m16.238s	9
10	Ralf Schumacher	Toyota	69 laps	2	1m15.534s	11
11	Rubens Barrichello	Honda	69 laps	2	1m15.761s	13
12	Mark Webber	Red Bull	69 laps	2	1m15.806s	14
13	David Coulthard	Red Bull	69 laps	2	no time	16
14	Alexander Wurz	Williams	69 laps	2	1m16.241s	18
15	Heikki Kovalainen	Renault	69 laps	3	1m15.826s	6
16	Takuma Sato	Super Aguri	68 laps	2	1m16.244s	22*
17	Adrian Sutil	Spyker	68 laps	3	1m17.915s	21
R	Scott Speed	Toro Rosso	55 laps/gearbox	2	1m16.049s	15
R	Christijan Albers	Spyker	28 laps/fuel rig attached	1	1m17.826s	20
R	Anthony Davidson	Super Aguri	1 lap/crash damage	0	1m16.366s	19
R	Jarno Trulli	Toyota	1 lap/crash damage	0	1m15.935s	8
R	Vitantonio Liuzzi	Toro Rosso	0 laps/accident	0	1m16.142s	17

FASTEST LAP: MASSA, 1M16.099S (129.661MPH/208.670KPH) ON LAP 42
RACE LEADERS: MASSA 1-19, 23-43; RAIKKONEN 20-22, 44-70
* DENOTES 10-PLACE GRID PENALTY FOR OVERTAKING UNDER WAVED YELLOW FLAGS IN US GP

TALKING POINT: THE ADVANTAGE SWINGS FERRARI'S WAY

With the F2007's relatively long wheelbase, it was always considered that its best hope lay with circuits with predominantly high-speed corners. Judging by its dominant form at Magny-Cours with the latest aerodynamic development parts fitted, this was proved correct as the Italian cars proved to be the class of the field rather than the McLarens that had ruled at twisty Montreal and Indianapolis. With fast, flowing Silverstone to follow, Raikkonen and Massa left the French GP with a smile on their faces, but ever-competitive McLaren struck back by saying that it wasn't too concerned. But they would say that, wouldn't they?

Ferrari gave Massa a car good enough for pole position, but it was his team-mate who triumphed.

BRITISH GP

The Great British Public wanted victory for their new hero Lewis Hamilton. He gave them pole, in highly dramatic style, but a win was two steps too far as Ferrari took control and McLaren's rookie had to settle for his ninth straight visit to the podium.

Ferrari's Kimi Raikkonen really got into his stride at Silverstone, while Lewis Hamilton started well but failed to live up to expectations.

One win good, two wins better, three wins great. That is certainly what Ferrari's Kimi Raikkonen must have thought as he rolled into parc ferme beneath the podium at Silverstone as his second straight win took him back into the championship battle, moving him up to third overall, one point ahead of his team-mate Felipe Massa.

Raikkonen had started second, and was unable to get ahead of Hamilton's McLaren on the run to the first corner, Copse. By veering away from the grid, Hamilton made sure of that and the crowd packing the grandstands and spectator banking loved it.

Hamilton stayed out front too, albeit with Raikkonen sitting right under his rear wing, but only for the 16 laps until he pitted. And this was the giveaway as he made his first stop two laps before Raikkonen made his from second place, and four laps before team-mate Fernando Alonso made his from third. Of the frontrunners, only BMW Sauber's Robert Kubica pitted on the same lap, from fourth. Once Hamilton had pulled into the pits, Raikkonen was immediately able to go up to 1s per lap faster, emphasising not only how much he'd been kept in check behind the McLaren but also just how hard it was to pass with the 2007 aerodynamic regulations as turbulent air affected the following car.

Missing from this group at this stage, though, was Massa whose engine had cut out on the grid, causing an aborted start and meaning that he had to start the race from last instead of from fourth. This scuppered his day, but certainly added to the occasion for the spectators as he ripped his way through the order. By the time of his pit stop on lap 20, he was up to second, albeit emerging in seventh.

After this round of stops, it was Alonso who led from Raikkonen, having been short-fuelled to ensure that he came out in front, with Hamilton back to third after he made a slip-up at his pit stop and tried to leave too soon, losing time in the process. Thereafter, he struggled as his tyres grained, losing as much as 1s per lap to the leading duo. He would go on to finish third, but Lewis was nigh on 40s down on the winner, owning up to having guessed wrong on how best to set up his car and learning that sheer speed is best combined with experience.

It was clear that Raikkonen had the legs

on Alonso and he took the lead when the Spaniard brought his McLaren in for its second pit stop. The Finn stayed out for fully six more laps, and this made the difference he needed as he sprinted out of the pits 3s in front. From then, it was a case of job done: the race was his, and the season's first three-time winner was back in the hunt.

Fourth place went to Robert Kubica, much to the delight of a large Polish contingent in the crowd, but he had to fight to keep it in the closing laps as Massa closed right in. Just a couple of seconds back, Nick Heidfeld claimed sixth in the second BMW Sauber.

Both Renaults finished in the points, Heikki Kovalainen ahead of Giancarlo Fisichella, but Renault's fall from championship success was marked by the fact that they had both been lapped.

So too were the three British drivers not christened Lewis, with Jenson Button and David Coulthard finishing in 10th and 11th positions respectively, while Anthony Davidson failed to go the distance, parking his Super Aguri after an early battle with the Hondas when the rear of his car started to scrape the track and he had to retire it. Ralf Schumacher had already parked up with a front-end handling problem which was a shame as he had qualified his Toyota a much improved sixth.

SILVERSTONE ROUND 09

Date: **8 July 2007** Laps: **59** Distance: **187.871 miles/302.350km**
Weather: **Warm and bright**

RACE RESULT

Position	Driver	Team	Result	Stops	Qualifying Time	Grid
1	**Kimi Räikkönen**	Ferrari	1h21m43.074s	2	1m20.099s	2
2	**Fernando Alonso**	McLaren	1h21m45.533s	2	1m20.147s	3
3	**Lewis Hamilton**	McLaren	1h22m22.447s	2	1m19.997s	1
4	**Robert Kubica**	BMW Sauber	1h22m36.393s	2	1m20.401s	5
5	**Felipe Massa**	Ferrari	1h22m37.137s	2	1m20.265s	4*
6	**Nick Heidfeld**	BMW Sauber	1h22m39.410s	2	1m20.894s	9
7	**Heikki Kovalainen**	Renault	58 laps	2	1m20.721s	7
8	**Giancarlo Fisichella**	Renault	58 laps	2	1m20.775s	8
9	**Rubens Barrichello**	Honda	58 laps	1	1m20.364s	14
10	**Jenson Button**	Honda	58 laps	1	1m21.335s	18
11	**David Coulthard**	Red Bull	58 laps	2	1m20.329s	12
12	**Nico Rosberg**	Williams	58 laps	2	1m21.219s	17
13	**Alexander Wurz**	Williams	58 laps	2	1m20.350s	13
14	**Takuma Sato**	Super Aguri	57 laps	2	1m22.045s	21*
15	**Christijan Albers**	Spyker	57 laps	2	1m22.589s	22
16	**Vitantonio Liuzzi**	Toro Rosso	53 laps/gearbox	2	1m20.823s	16
R	**Jarno Trulli**	Toyota	43 laps/handling	2	1m21.240s	10
R	**Anthony Davidson**	Super Aguri	35 laps/handling	1	1m21.228s	19
R	**Scott Speed**	Toro Rosso	29 laps/accident	1	1m20.515s	15
R	**Ralf Schumacher**	Toyota	22 laps/handling	1	1m20.516s	6
R	**Adrian Sutil**	Spyker	16 laps/engine	0	1m22.019s	20
R	**Mark Webber**	Red Bull	8 laps/differential	0	1m20.235s	11

FASTEST LAP: RAIKKONEN, 1M20.638S (142.643MPH/229.562KPH) ON LAP 17*
RACE LEADERS: HAMILTON, 1-15; RAIKKONEN, 16-17, 38-59; ALONSO, 18-37
* DENOTES STARTED FROM THE PITLANE

TALKING POINT: FERRARI POINTS THE FINGER AT McLAREN

The talk of the paddock was one of the most contentious matters for years: industrial espionage. It wasn't the first time in recent years, as several ex-Ferrari employees were found guilty of taking drawings with them to Toyota. This time, the person being accused was McLaren's chief designer Mike Coughlan, who was found to be in possession of Ferrari drawings. It was thought that they had been sent to him by Nigel Stepney who was unsettled at Ferrari and had since been sacked, but nothing had been proved. Honda was implicated, but it was only after the FIA hearing on 26 July that the outcome was known and McLaren was given a conditional pardon.

Sacked Ferrari employee Nigel Stepney was in the news, as was McLaren's Mike Coughlan.

EUROPEAN GP

This was a belter, the best race of the year. It was wet, it was unpredictable and it was exciting from lights to chequered flag. At the end, Fernando Alonso emerged a delighted winner, but only after barging past Felipe Massa in the dying laps.

A perplexed Massa, a satisfied Alonso and a delighted Mark Webber share the podium.

Lewis Hamilton needed to re-establish himself after Raikkonen's double for Ferrari at Magny-Cours then Silverstone. With the layout better suited to the McLaren, thanks to its medium-speed bends and the fact that Lewis had dominated the GP2 races there in 2006, he had reason to be optimistic.

He topped the timesheets in first practice with only Raikkonen outpacing him before qualifying. All was looking good for Hamilton until early in the final segment of qualifying when it all went wrong (see right).

This left the way clear for Raikkonen to take pole ahead of Fernando Alonso, Felipe Massa, Nick Heidfeld and Robert Kubica, with the sidelined Hamilton demoted to 10th place, providing that he was given the go-ahead by the FIA to start the race.

The sky was dark as the cars formed up on the grid, but it was dry as Raikkonen accelerated into the lead, with Massa making it a Ferrari one-two as he demoted Alonso. Famed for his first lap overtaking, Hamilton passed both Toyotas, Mark Webber's Red Bull and Heikki Kovalainen's Renault by Turn 1. Then he was gifted two more positions out of Turn 2 when the BMWs clashed, but the spinning Kubica clipped him and he picked up a puncture. Yet, as Hamilton drove slowly back to the pits, it started to pour.

Treaded tyres were needed, but Raikkonen nearly spun in the pit entrance and was forced to miss it, lumbering himself with a further lap in very wet conditions on dry weather tyres.

One driver had reason to smile and this was debutant Markus Winkelhock whose Spyker team had been tipped off that rain might hit and had brought him in before the start to change to intermediates. As he was starting last, it was a gamble worth taking and a gamble that paid off as he found himself leading his first Formula One race when he passed Raikkonen halfway around the second lap.

Turn 1 was waterlogged as the field raced onto lap 3. Winkelhock got around it fine, but he had the advantage of having pitted and put on full wets. Massa and Alonso almost lost it there, but behind them car after car aquaplaned off, with Jenson Button slithering out of fourth place after an inspired climb from 17th.

By the time Hamilton emerged on intermediates, he was faced with a car park of cars that had slid off. And he joined them... The difference was, Lewis kept his engine going and was craned out, losing a lap in the process.

The race was red-flagged and it was half an hour before it was restarted, with the safety car leading the field around. Winkelhock was passed the moment it withdrew, with Massa being chased by Alonso and the Red Bulls next up ahead of the Renaults.

By lap 13, almost everyone had changed to dry tyres, but a charging Raikkonen was given a helping hand when Webber slid wide on rejoining and he shot into third place. The Finn was unable to capitalise, though, as he retired with a hydraulic problem.

It still looked as though it was to be Ferrari's day, as Alonso was struggling to get his car to handle in the dry and had lost 8s to Massa.

The best was saved to last, though, and it came after the rain returned with eight laps to go. Alonso had hunted Massa down and five laps from home dived up the inside of the Brazilian at the Ford Kurve. They clashed, but the McLaren came out ahead and raced on to win. They exchanged angry words afterwards.

Alonso was ecstatic, not only to have won, but to have cut his points deficit to just two as his team-mate's bid to salvage points came up just short. Hamilton had passed Fisichella for ninth on the final lap, but ended up just 1.5s short of Kovalainen.

The final place on the podium went to Webber, to give Red Bull Racing reason for a rare smile. In fact, they had two reasons to do so, as David Coulthard had used all of his experience to work his way up to fifth. However, Webber had only just managed to hang on as Alex Wurz – another driver who shines in topsy-turvy races – was just 0.2s behind as they crossed the finish line.

NURBURGRING ROUND 10
Date: **22 July 2007** Laps: **60** Distance: **191.880 miles/308.802km**
Weather: **Overcast and wet**

RACE RESULT

Position	Driver	Team	Result	Stops	Qualifying Time	Grid
1	Fernando Alonso	McLaren	2h06m26.358s	4	1m31.741s	2
2	Felipe Massa	Ferrari	2h06m34.513s	4	1m31.778s	3
3	Mark Webber	Red Bull	2h07m32.032s	4	1m32.476s	6
4	Alexander Wurz	Williams	2h07m32.295s	4	1m31.996s	12
5	David Coulthard	Red Bull	2h07m40.014s	4	1m33.151s	20
6	Nick Heidfeld	BMW Sauber	2h07m46.656s	6	1m31.840s	4
7	Robert Kubica	BMW Sauber	2h07m48.773s	4	1m32.123s	5
8	Heikki Kovalainen	Renault	59 laps	4	1m32.478s	7
9	Lewis Hamilton	McLaren	59 laps	4	1m33.833s	10
10	Giancarlo Fisichella	Renault	59 laps	4	1m32.010s	13
11	Rubens Barrichello	Honda	59 laps	5	1m32.221s	14
12	Anthony Davidson	Super Aguri	59 laps	6	1m32.451s	15
13	Jarno Trulli	Toyota	59 laps	6	1m32.501s	8
R	Kimi Räikkönen	Ferrari	34 laps/hydraulics	2	1m31.450s	1
R	Takuma Sato	Super Aguri	19 laps/hydraulics	3	1m32.838s	16
R	Ralf Schumacher	Toyota	18 laps/collision	3	1m32.570s	9
R	Markus Winkelhock	Spyker	13 laps/hydraulics	2	1m35.940s	22
R	Jenson Button	Honda	2 laps/spun off	1	1m32.983s	17
R	Adrian Sutil	Spyker	2 laps/spun off	1	1m34.500s	21
R	Nico Rosberg	Williams	2 laps/spun off	1	1m31.978s	11
R	Scott Speed	Toro Rosso	2 laps/spun off	1	1m33.038s	18
R	Vitantonio Liuzzi	Toro Rosso	2 laps/spun off	2	1m33.148s	19

FASTEST LAP: FELIPE MASSA, 1M32.853S (124.020MPH/199.592KPH) ON LAP 34
LAP LEADERS: RAIKKONEN 1; WINKELHOCK 2-7; MASSA 8-12, 14-55; COULTHARD 13; ALONSO 56-60

TALKING POINT: HAMILTON SET BACK BY MASSIVE SHUNT

There are moments when racing can take your breath away and this did just that to Lewis Hamilton. It came at Turn 8 at the start of the final qualifying session, and Lewis was a passenger as his McLaren failed to negotiate the left-hander, bouncing across the gravel before piling into the tyre wall. Stretchered to the medical centre, it took a while before news broke that his crash had been caused by a wheel coming loose and its tyre being cut following a problem with a wheelgun and then, more importantly, that Lewis was unhurt. It took medical clearance before he was allowed to race, but at least his season hadn't been hijacked.

Hamilton slammed into the barriers in qualifying and yet still could have finished third in the race.

HUNGARIAN GP

The spectre of industrial espionage hung heavy over Ferrari and McLaren when the teams arrived in Hungary, but McLaren's woes doubled in qualifying before Lewis Hamilton held off Kimi Raikkonen to bring the team cheer by winning.

Budapest is a wonderful city to visit at any time of year. But in a summer that was a luke-warm wash-out for Northern Europeans, the sun-drenched banks of the River Danube were particularly appealing. Unless you were caught up in the Ferrari-McLaren spying scandal... It had rumbled from July to August and the prevalent feeling in Formula One was that it would be best for all concerned to just get on with the racing.

Formula One being as it is, though, this wasn't to be the case. As if intentionally to give McLaren team chief Ron Dennis one last, giant headache before he headed off for his summer break, his ultra-competitive drivers elected to make life difficult for themselves in qualifying. First off, Lewis Hamilton declined instructions to let Fernando Alonso through at the start of the third qualifying session. His reasoning was that Ferrari's Kimi Raikkonen was right on the Spaniard's tail and would probably try to force his way past at the same time, thus compromising his lapping.

This was a case of trucculent disobedience, but it didn't affect Alonso's track position or lap time. But, what Alonso did to Hamilton in the dying seconds most certainly did...

Alonso came into the pits for his final refuelling and change of rubber. Hamilton was instructed to slow his in-lap and then report at the pits at the same. He arrived, sat waiting, saw Alonso's lollipop be lifted but then became incredulous, as did the mechanics, as Alonso didn't budge for a further 10 seconds and then blasted off to complete his out-lap with seconds to go

Hamilton triumphed after a topsy-turvy meeting, chased all the way by Raikkonen's Ferrari.

before the chequered flag fell, thus being able to put in a final flying lap to knock Hamilton off pole. Having been made to wait so, Hamilton was never going to be able to get onto his planned final flier.

So, it was time for Dennis to go on the defensive again, this time down to his laudable modus operandi of allowing his drivers to race each other rather than adopt the Jean Todt style of primacy for a lead driver at Ferrari. The press were at first confused by the conflicting stories from the drivers and then had a field day. The FIA deliberated until just short of midnight before penalising Alonso five grid positions for impeding Hamilton and electing that McLaren's drivers would be able to score

points in the race, but that the team would collect none.

All of this obscured the fact that Hamilton appeared to be right back on form after his first ever non-score a fortnight earlier at the European GP. Nick Heidfeld would be lining up on the outside of the front row, promoted by Alonso's demotion, with Raikkonen delighted to not only have moved up a place to third but also from the dirty, pitwall side of the grid. His would be the only Ferrari in a position to challenge, as Felipe Massa had failed to advance from second qualifying as his crew forgot to refuel his car and he lost considerable time as his car was pushed back up the pit lane.

At the start, Raikkonen was able to

outdrag Heidfeld to slot into second behind Hamilton. Nico Rosberg and Ralf Schumacher claimed fourth and fifth into the first corner, with the Williams driver giving Alonso a chop that caused the McLaren driver to lift and stay behind the pair and then lose a place to Robert Kubica at the tightish right-hander. To make matters worse, Alonso slid wide at the final corner and Mark Webber demoted him too. It took Alonso three laps to undo this mess and move back to sixth, where he lost time stuck behind Schumacher.

Hamilton had the upper hand over Raikkonen in the first stint. Both pitted on the same lap, but there was no chance of a change of position. The second stint was better for Raikkonen and he closed right in, but he pitted four laps before Hamilton and was 4s behind when the British driver rejoined. Fast he was, faster than Hamilton actually, but he could find no way past.

As overtaking is all but impossible at the Hungaroring, several runners opted for three pit stops, including Heidfeld, who was pressed at every corner by Alonso in the final laps, but hung on.

Emphasising how hard it is to overtake, Massa started 14th and finished 13th, which was the polar opposite of his drive through the field in Australia from the back of the grid to sixth place.

HUNGARORING ROUND 11
Date: **5 August 2007** Laps: **70** Distance: **190.511 miles/306.598km**
Weather: **Hot and bright**

RACE RESULT

Position	Driver	Team	Result	Stops	Qualifying Time	Grid
1	**Lewis Hamilton**	McLaren	1h35m52.991s	2	1m19.781s	1
2	**Kimi Räikkönen**	Ferrari	1h35m53.706s	2	1m20.410s	3
3	**Nick Heidfeld**	BMW Sauber	1h36m36.120s	3	1m20.259s	2
4	**Fernando Alonso**	McLaren	1h36m37.849s	2	1m19.674s	6*
5	**Robert Kubica**	BMW Sauber	1h36m40.607s	3	1m20.876s	7
6	**Ralf Schumacher**	Toyota	1h36m43.660s	2	1m20.714s	5
7	**Nico Rosberg**	Williams	1h36m52.130s	3	1m20.632s	4
8	**Heikki Kovalainen**	Renault	1h37m01.095s	2	1m20.779s	11
9	**Mark Webber**	Red Bull	1h37m09.322s	3	1m21.256s	9
10	**Jarno Trulli**	Toyota	69 laps	2	1m21.206s	8
11	**David Coulthard**	Red Bull	69 laps	2	1m20.718s	10
12	**Giancarlo Fisichella**	Renault	69 laps	2	1m21.079s	13*
13	**Felipe Massa**	Ferrari	69 laps	2	1m21.021s	14
14	**Alexander Wurz**	Williams	69 laps	2	1m20.865s	12
15	**Takuma Sato**	Super Aguri	69 laps	2	1m22.143s	19
16	**Sebastian Vettel**	Toro Rosso	69 laps	2	1m22.177s	20
17	**Adrian Sutil**	Spyker	68 laps	2	1m22.737s	21
18	**Rubens Barrichello**	Honda	68 laps	2	1m21.877s	18
R	**Vitantonio Liuzzi**	Toro Rosso	42 laps/electronics	1	1m21.993s	16
R	**Anthony Davidson**	Super Aguri	41 laps/accident	1	1m21.127s	15
R	**Jenson Button**	Honda	35 laps/throttle sensor	1	1m21.737s	17
R	**Sakon Yamamoto**	Spyker	4 laps/accident	0	1m23.774s	22

FASTEST LAP: RAIKKONEN, 1M20.047S (122.428MPH/197.029KPH) ON LAP 70
RACE LEADERS: HAMILTON, 1-70
* DENOTES FIVE-PLACE GRID PENALTY

TALKING POINT: VETTEL LANDS A DRIVE AS SPEED IS FIRED

There was little love lost at Toro Rosso after both cars ended up in the gravel after two laps of the European GP. Scott Speed said that he had a tussle with team boss Franz Tost. With the scene already tense between the drivers and the management, Speed was found to be surplus to requirements as parent company Red Bull had Sebastian Vettel under long-term contract and needed to place him in a race seat for 2008 rather than keep him as BMW test driver. So he arrived in Hungary in Speed's car. Vitantonio Liuzzi was also feeling the pressure as Champ Car champion Sebastien Bourdais was being lined up for STR's other race seat for 2008.

New weekend, new overalls, as Vettel moved from BMW Sauber to replace Scott Speed at Toro Rosso.

TURKISH GP

To get back into the hunt, Ferrari needed to win at the Turkish Grand Prix, and this is what they did as their drivers made the most of starting on the clean side of the grid and assumed a one-two running order that was never overturned, with Massa winning.

Massa leads Raikkonen, Hamilton and Kubica into Turn 1 and would go on to win the race.

The Istanbul circuit has a special place in Felipe Massa's heart. Not, as you might think, simply because it is one of the most challenging the drivers visit, but because it was the scene of his maiden grand prix success in 2006. Think then how much more Felipe must love it now, having made it two wins on the trot there to not only score his first win since the Spanish GP in May, but also to move him back ahead of his Ferrari team-mate Kimi Raikkonen in their pursuit of McLaren's Lewis Hamilton and Fernando Alonso in the points table. In a battle that was swinging between McLaren and Ferrari, this one was Ferrari's and gave him hope, confidence and a gigantic smile.

Lewis Hamilton had given it his best shot to pip Massa to pole position, but had failed by 0.044s, with Fernando Alonso behind third fastest qualifier Kimi Raikkonen by an even smaller amount. What was going to be interesting was to see which of these would call in for their first pit stop ahead of their rivals. Massa led away and his race was made easier by Raikkonen jumping Hamilton for second place as they accelerated away from the grid. Starting on the clean side of the grid was a help for both red cars.

If this was frustrating for Hamilton, it was worse still for Alonso as it allowed Robert Kubica to demote him, followed by Nick Heidfeld later in the opening lap. This was to cost the Spaniard dear as he failed to repass them in his opening stint, losing him probably 10 seconds.

Of the frontrunners, Raikkonen was the first to pit, followed in on the same lap by the frustrated Alonso. Massa was next in a lap later, one before Hamilton, suggesting that had Hamilton been fuelled one lap lighter for his qualifying shot, he might have nabbed pole, the clean side of the track and perhaps been leading.

As it was, everything went Ferrari's way as Massa and Raikkonen ran one-two through the second stint and were then given a bonus when Hamilton picked up a delaminated front tyre three laps ahead of his planned second stop, not only losing him laps with a light fuel load, but forcing him to limp back to the pits. This dropped him to fifth, where he would finish. So Alonso and Heidfeld were promoted to third and fourth.

While Massa was able to cruise to the third win of his campaign, Raikkonen was keen to show that he might have won had he managed to get ahead, something that he tried before their second round of pit stops, causing Massa to run wide at Turn 7 as he defended his position. The move failed, but Raikkonen dropped back in the closing laps and then banged in appreciably the fastest lap of the race, by 0.6s, just to show what might have been. He later complained of the difficulty to overtake in F1 these days. Had he not run wide with two corners to go on his final qualifying flier, pole might have been his and so he wouldn't have had to...

Heikki Kovalainen was the better placed Renault driver for the fourth race in a row, finishing sixth, with Giancarlo Fisichella 13s behind in ninth. Between them, Nico Rosberg and Kubica bagged sixth and eighth, with the Williams driver pleased with continuing progress and the Pole scuppered by having to pit early for each of his stops after starting with the lightest fuel load of all.

One remarkable feature of the Turkish GP was that all but one of the cars finished, with only Mark Webber's Red Bull dropping out, after an accident on lap 10 caused by a hydraulic failure. He had been running 10th at the time behind team-mate David Coulthard, confident that his heavy starting fuel load would have helped him up the order as the race ran its course. Coulthard, up from 13th after a flying start, would go on to finish 10th, demoted by Fisichella who had a first lap clash with Jarno Trulli's Toyota on the way into Turn 1.

Another performance of note was Anthony Davidson's for Super Aguri. He qualified an impressive 11th and went to on finish 14th for the still under-funded team after being pushed back on the opening lap as he avoided the spinning Trulli and then clipped another car in the melee and struggled with affected handling thereafter.

ISTANBUL PARK ROUND 12

Date: **26 August 2007** Laps: **58** Distance: **192.388 miles/309.619km**
Weather: **Hot and bright**

RACE RESULT

Position	Driver	Team	Result	Stops	Qualifying Time	Grid
1	Felipe Massa	Ferrari	1h26m42.161s	2	1m27.329s	1
2	Kimi Räikkönen	Ferrari	1h26m44.436s	2	1m27.546s	3
3	Fernando Alonso	McLaren	1h27m08.342s	2	1m27.574s	4
4	Nick Heidfeld	BMW Sauber	1h27m21.835s	2	1m28.037s	6
5	Lewis Hamilton	McLaren	1h27m27.246s	2	1m27.373s	2
6	Heikki Kovalainen	Renault	1h27m28.330s	2	1m28.491s	7
7	Nico Rosberg	Williams	1h27m37.939s	2	1m28.501s	8
8	Robert Kubica	BMW Sauber	1h27m38.868s	2	1m27.722s	5
9	Giancarlo Fisichella	Renault	1h27m41.652s	2	1m29.322s	10
10	David Coulthard	Red Bull	1h27m53.170s	2	1m28.100s	13
11	Alexander Wurz	Williams	1h28m01.789s	2	1m28.390s	15
12	Ralf Schumacher	Toyota	57 laps	1	1m28.809s	17
13	Jenson Button	Honda	57 laps	2	1m28.220s	22*
14	Anthony Davidson	Super Aguri	57 laps	2	1m28.002s	11
15	Vitantonio Liuzzi	Toro Rosso	57 laps	2	1m28.798s	16
16	Jarno Trulli	Toyota	57 laps	2	1m28.740s	9
17	Rubens Barrichello	Honda	57 laps	2	1m28.188s	14
18	Takuma Sato	Super Aguri	57 laps	1	1m28.953s	18
19	Sebastian Vettel	Toro Rosso	57 laps	2	1m29.408s	19
20	Sakon Yamamoto	Spyker	56 laps	2	1m31.479s	21
21	Adrian Sutil	Spyker	53 laps	2	1m29.861s	20
R	Mark Webber	Red Bull	9 laps/hydraulics	0	1m28.013s	12

FASTEST LAP: RAIKKONEN, 1M27.295S (136.815MPH/220.183KPH) ON LAP 57
RACE LEADERS: MASSA, 1-19, 22-42, 44-58, HAMILTON 23, KOVALAINEN 24, ALONSO 43
* INCLUDES 10-PLACE GRID PENALTY

TALKING POINT: ALONSO REMAINS UNHAPPY AT McLAREN

Formula One's summer break was supposed to soothe troubled minds. But, just in case, McLaren called a peace meeting between its at-war drivers Alonso and Hamilton on the Thursday before the Turkish GP. All parties reckoned that the problems that arose during qualifying for the Hungarian GP were behind them. However, Alonso then told Spanish newspapers that he still wasn't happy, that as a double world champion he deserved more respect, most especially as he had brought to the team half a second' and made it competitive again. This infuriated the team as it felt the gains had come from team work from many departments.

Smiles were hard to come by as Fernando Alonso found himself under even increasing media scrutiny.

ITALIAN GP

The atmosphere in the paddock at Monza was described as toxic as the spying scandal dragged on, but McLaren did everything it could to keep its focus on the racing and came away with a one-two result for Alonso ahead of Hamilton on Ferrari's home turf.

McLaren was back on top on Ferrari's home ground and Fernando Alonso was always in control as he raced to victory ahead of Lewis Hamilton.

Sport and politics should never be mixed, so it was with increasing anger that the teams found themselves under the spotlight at Monza. McLaren was racing under the shadow of what might be meted out to them the following Thursday when the FIA's World Motor Sport Council sat in Paris to decide its fate in the spying scandal.

Despite a judiciously-timed visit from Italian legal authorities on Saturday, McLaren qualified first and second, with Fernando Alonso on pole by 0.037s. With the Ferraris third (Felipe Massa) and fifth (Kimi Raikkonen) behind Nick Heidfeld's BMW Sauber, there was some joy at least, even though the Finn being more than 1s off pole suggested that he had been running

with a far heavier fuel load and might be able to spring a strategical surprise.

Any hope that Hamilton had of outdragging Alonso appeared to have gone when he was passed by Massa and, almost, by Raikkonen. However, he's nothing if not brave and simply drove around the outside of the lead Ferrari under braking into the chicane. It looked as though he might pass Alonso too, but his McLaren then received a thump up the back from Massa and was put across the kerbs.

A lap later, there was more pushing and shoving at the first chicane, with David Coulthard coming off worst as his nose was loosened against the rear of Giancarlo Fisichella's Renault and then folded back

under the car as he accelerated away from the chicane, giving him no steering as he entered the Curva Grande at 150mph.0

Coulthard's crash brought out the safety car and this offered Hamilton another crack at Alonso when it returned to the pits, but Alonso is nothing if not wily and not only held him at bay but appeared to try and slow his team-mate sufficiently at the first chicane so that Massa might catch him.

As it was, Hamilton held onto second place and this is how the pair stayed to the finish, even taking into account Raikkonen's best efforts as he one-stopped the race. In fact, after a second stint spoiled by vibrations from a flat-spotted tyre, Hamilton emerged behind the Finn, but he attacked like a fury while his new tyres were at their best and Raikkonen simply had no answer as he scythed by into the first chicane two laps later.

To make matters worse for Ferrari, Massa failed to score, having become the race's only other retirement when a handling problem that he thought at first had been caused by a rear puncture proved terminal. It was found to be a broken damper.

So, this left the way clear for BMW Sauber to snaffle fourth and fifth, Nick Heidfeld leading home Robert Kubica. Proving that solid progress was being made by Williams, Nico Rosberg rose from eighth to sixth for his third straight points finish, having used his one-stop strategy to pass Heikki Kovalainen. Rosberg also fought with Kubica, but could do nothing to hold him back when the Pole rocketed past him at the first chicane after a slow pit stop in which his car fell off its jack.

The final point went to Jenson Button and it was a rare chance for the English driver to smile in a troubled year, as it was only his second points score. He had qualified 10th and benefited from Jarno Trulli making a terrible start and then from Massa retiring. However, he enjoyed a tussle with Rosberg in the first stint, albeit hampered by a flat-spotted front tyre.

MONZA ROUND 13

Date: **9 September 2007** Laps: **53** Distance: **190.587 miles/ 306.720km** Weather: **Warm and bright**

RACE RESULT

Position	Driver	Team	Result	Stops	Qualifying Time	Grid
1	Fernando Alonso	McLaren	1h18m37.806s	2	1m21.997s	1
2	Lewis Hamilton	McLaren	1h18m43.868s	2	1m22.034s	2
3	Kimi Räikkönen	Ferrari	1h19m05.131s	1	1m23.183s	5
4	Nick Heidfeld	BMW Sauber	1h19m34.368s	2	1m23.174s	4
5	Robert Kubica	BMW Sauber	1h19m38.364s	2	1m23.446s	6
6	Nico Rosberg	Williams	1h19m43.616s	1	1m24.382s	8
7	Heikki Kovalainen	Renault	1h19m44.557s	2	1m24.102s	7
8	Jenson Button	Honda	1h19m49.974s	1	1m25.165s	10
9	Mark Webber	Red Bull	1h19m53.685s	1	1m23.166s	11
10	Rubens Barrichello	Honda	1h19m54.764s	1	1m23.176s	12
11	Jarno Trulli	Toyota	1h19m55.542s	1	1m24.555s	9
12	Giancarlo Fisichella	Renault	52 laps	1	1m23.325s	15
13	Alexander Wurz	Williams	52 laps	1	1m23.209s	13
14	Anthony Davidson	Super Aguri	52 laps	1	1m23.274s	14
15	Ralf Schumacher	Toyota	52 laps	1	1m23.787s	18
16	Takuma Sato	Super Aguri	52 laps	1	1m23.749s	17
17	Vitantonio Liuzzi	Toro Rosso	52 laps	1	1m23.886s	19
18	Sebastian Vettel	Toro Rosso	52 laps	2	1m23.351s	16
19	Adrian Sutil	Spyker	52 laps	2	1m24.699s	21
20	Sakon Yamamoto	Spyker	52 laps	2	1m25.084s	22
R	Felipe Massa	Ferrari	10/suspension	1	1m22.549s	3
R	David Coulthard	Red Bull	1/collision	0	1m24.019s	20

FASTEST LAP: ALONSO, 1M22.871S, 156.370MPH/251.653KPH ON LAP 15
RACE LEADERS: ALONSO, 1-20, 26-53; RAIKKONEN, 21-25

TALKING POINT: FORMULA ONE SEEKS TO INCREASE OVERTAKING

In contrast to the spying scandal, a more worthwhile matter was discussed at Monza: ways of ensuring that there is more overtaking. The FIA Overtaking Working Group met to formulate ways to improve the show after analysing factors in the Fondmetal windtunnel. Comprising Ferrari's (Rory Byrne), McLaren's (Paddy Lowe) and Renault's (Pat Symonds), the OWG came up with ideas such as a new diffuser that should enable drivers to run behind another car more easily, with a view to announcing changes that need to be made to the rules for 2009 to offer more of a spectacle.

Getting close to the car ahead through the Parabolica is the key to overtaking at the first chicane.

BELGIAN GP

Ferrari, gifted the lead in the constructors' championship, came away with a one-two on Formula One's return to Spa-Francorchamps, but almost nobody was talking about the racing as the spying scandal continued to dominate everything.

Raikkonen drove beautifully to triumph on a weekend when sport was overshadowed by politics.

Talk of the court proceedings in Paris and outrage at the size of the fine meted out to McLaren (see box-out) took precedence over almost all else in Belgium, which was a shame if you were Ferrari as it reduced the impact of a markedly strong one-two finish and also for lovers of the greatest tracks visited by Formula One as it should have been a celebration of the greatest of them all, Spa-Francorchamps.

The run to the first corner at Spa, the right-hand La Source hairpin, is always tight, but the McLaren drivers contrived to make it harder still, as Alonso appeared to be tripped up slightly when Massa got a little sideways and then drove across to the track's edge to block Hamilton's attack down the outside, putting the Brit over the kerbs. Hamilton wasn't finished, though, and the pair ran side-by-side down the hill towards Eau Rouge.

They were still side-by-side midway through the fearsome corner, before Hamilton chose discretion over valour and backed off.

So, Raikkonen led up the hill to Les Combes from Massa, Alonso and Hamilton, with Rosberg fifth and a fast-starting Heikki Kovalainen up to sixth. This was bad news for Mark Webber and Heidfeld, as it meant that they were to be delayed by the Renault, as it was heavier, running a one-stop strategy. They would both pass the Finn, but it helped Rosberg make good his escape.

The best start of all was made from near the rear of the grid, with Adrian Sutil blasting his new, B-spec Spyker from 19th to 14th by making the most of starting on the soft tyre and blasting flat through Eau Rouge on lap 1 to outdrag his rivals up the hill that followed. He hassled David Coulthard's Red Bull for a while, something that certainly wasn't in the Scot's script, but then again neither was retiring with hydraulic failure when in with a shot of the final point. Eventually, having run as 12th, Sutil had to settle for 14th, but he'd done enough to remind people that as the driver who pressed Lewis Hamilton when they were team-mates in European Formula Three, he's worth watching.

Another driver on the move was Robert Kubica who was having to make up ground after starting 14th due to a 10-place grid penalty for his team having changed his engine. The Pole was up to 10th after two laps, then deposed Ralf Schumacher and Kovalainen before the first of his two pit stops, but he was unable to advance further than ninth as Kovalainen's one-stop strategy dropped him back one of the places gained.

So, with Ferrari supreme at the front, and

McLaren easily the best of the rest, it was left to Heidfeld to claim fifth place, having passed Rosberg by running a considerably longer opening stint. By the end, Rosberg was 25s adrift, and just 4s clear of Webber, with Kovalainen a further 5s back, with Kubica right under his rear wing.

Tenth place went to Schumacher, with his Toyota team-mate Jarno Trulli next up. this emphasised how the Japanese team continues to fill the middle ground. Starting from eighth and running a two-stop strategy, Trulli ought to have finished at the tail-end of the points, but he lost ground at the first corner on the opening lap and was then delayed by running behind the heavier cars of team-mate Schumacher and Coulthard. His problem in overtaking two palpably slower cars emphasised why so much research is being put into making it easier for cars to overtake, as 2007's cars appear to have been the worst ever in this aspect.

At some grands prix, drivers realise that nothing is going to go right for them. Take Renault's Giancarlo Fisichella at Spa. He just missed out on getting into Q3, then ended up at the back of the grid after an engine change. He then swapped to the T-car and started from the pit lane, but his race was short as he crashed on the opening lap, damaging his R27's suspension.

SPA-FRANCORCHAMPS ROUND 14
Date: **16 September 2007** Laps: **44** Distance: **191.491 miles/ 308.175km** Weather: **Warm and bright**

RACE RESULT

Position	Driver	Team	Result	Stops	Qualifying Time	Grid
1	**Kimi Räikkönen**	Ferrari	1h20m39.066s	2	1m45.994s	1
2	**Felipe Massa**	Ferrari	1h20m43.761s	2	1m46.011s	2
3	**Fernando Alonso**	McLaren	1h20m53.409s	2	1m46.091s	3
4	**Lewis Hamilton**	McLaren	1h21m02.681s	2	1m46.406s	4
5	**Nick Heidfeld**	BMW Sauber	1h21m30.945s	2	1m47.409s	6
6	**Nico Rosberg**	Williams	1h21m55.942s	2	1m47.334s	5
7	**Mark Webber**	Red Bull	1h21m59.705s	2	1m47.524s	7
8	**Heikki Kovalainen**	Renault	1h22m04.172s	1	1m48.505s	9
9	**Robert Kubica**	BMW Sauber	1h22m04.727s	2	1m46.996s	14*
10	**Ralf Schumacher**	Toyota	1h22m07.640s	1	1m46.618s	10
11	**Jarno Trulli**	Toyota	1h22m22.719s	2	1m47.798s	8
12	**Vitantonio Liuzzi**	Toro Rosso	43 laps	1	1m47.115s	13
13	**Rubens Barrichello**	Honda	43 laps	1	1m47.954s	17
14	**Adrian Sutil**	Spyker	43 laps	2	1m48.044s	19
15	**Takuma Sato**	Super Aguri	43 laps	2	1m47.980s	18
16	**Anthony Davidson**	Super Aguri	43 laps	1	1m48.199s	20**
17	**Sakon Yamamoto**	Spyker	43 laps	2	1m49.577s	21
	Jenson Button	Honda	36 laps/hydraulics	1	1m46.955s	12
R	**Alexander Wurz**	Williams	34 laps/fuel pressure	2	1m47.394s	15
R	**David Coulthard**	Red Bull	29 laps/throttle	1	1m46.800s	11
R	**Sebastian Vettel**	Toro Rosso	8 laps/steering	1	1m47.581s	16
R	**Giancarlo Fisichella**	Renault	1 lap/suspension	0	1m46.603s	22***

FASTEST LAP: MASSA, 1M48.036S, 145.021MPH/233.389KPH ON LAP 34
RACE LEADERS: RAIKKONEN X-44
* TEN-PLACE GRID PENALTY ** STARTED FROM THE PITLANE *** 10-PLACE GRID PENALTY AND THEN STARTED FROM THE PITLANE

TALKING POINT: McLAREN LOSES POINTS AND A LOT OF MONEY

There was intense speculation before the Belgian GP over the outcome of the World Motor Sport Council meeting to consider McLaren's role in the spying scandal. When it came, with a $100m fine and the loss of the team's points (it had been leading Ferrari 166 to 143), there was a sharp intake of breath. Even more so when it became clear that it took persuasion from Bernie Ecclestone to stop it from being banned for 2008. FIA President Max Mosley said "it was only when I received information from the Italian police that there had been 323 SMS messages between Coughlan and Stepney that I concluded there had to be more to this case."

McLaren's Ron Dennis faces up to questioning outside court in Paris, feeling $100m less well off.

JAPANESE GP

Conditions were foul, track conditions treacherous and visibility next to neglible, but Lewis Hamilton was in control from start to finish and his victory here, combined with Fernando Alonso's retirement, left him on the brink of the title.

Taking his first grand prix win in Canada in June was a landmark, but Lewis Hamilton's win on Formula One's return to Fuji was all about delivering when the pressure was on.

Having arrived with just a two-point lead over increasingly fierce rival Fernando Alonso, Lewis re-established momentum by securing pole by the smallest of margins.

Being in front gives an advantage, but it was the ultimate advantage in the fog and rain, as Lewis was the only driver other than the one driving the safety car leading them around after the start who could see.

Neither Ferrari had fitted extreme wets, as requested by the FIA, the team claiming that the message was never received. One glance at the conditions might have dictated that this was wise, but the outcome was that Massa spun on lap 1 and pitted for extreme wets, something that Raikkonen did on lap 2, dropping both to the tail of the field. Raikkonen added a further spin on lap 6.

On lap 19, with the rain easing, the safety car withdrew. Yet there was immediately trouble behind as Heidfeld and Button touched, and Heidfeld's spin triggered a bunching of the field that caused a collision between Wurz and Massa, removing Wurz on the spot and earning Massa a drive-through.

Hamilton made a break ahead of Alonso, with Sebastian Vettel holding third for Toro Rosso. He'd qualified eighth, by going out with a car set up for the wet rather than using the dry set-ups that many of his rivals had used in qualifying as they believed race day would be dry. Webber was next, followed by Button, Fisichella, Kovalainen and Kubica.

Button's hopes of glory were thwarted on lap 23 when he had to pit for a new nose.

Alonso pitted from second on lap 27. Hamilton came in from the lead a lap later. This left Vettel in front ahead of Webber. Hamilton took over when they pitted.

When Vettel made his stop, Kubica dived past Kovalainen. Two laps later, Kubica pitched Hamilton into a spin. Then Alonso clashed with Vettel and had a spin.

Kovalainen took over when Webber came

A flawless victory in the rain and gloom at Fuji Speedway put Lewis Hamilton on the verge of clinching the world title in his maiden season.

in, leading from Fisichella and Coulthard, with Hamilton fourth. On lap 38, this became second as Kovalainen and Coulthard pitted. Three laps later, Hamilton was back in the lead when Fisichella came in, while Kubica was called in for a drive-through penalty.

Then the battle was reshaped when Alonso crashed and brought out the safety car. His retirement left Hamilton leading Webber, the Toro Rossos of Vettel and Liuzzi, Kovalainen and Massa. Liuzzi pitted on lap 44, two laps before Vettel ran into the back of Webber.

When racing resumed, Hamilton dropped Kovalainen, with Massa next from Coulthard, but Raikkonen was flying and passed Coulthard. He took third when Massa pitted.

Hamilton was 12s clear and able to win as he pleased, with Kovalainen having to hold off Raikkonen for a first podium finish.

Hamilton's win, combined with Alonso's failure, left him 12 points clear with 20 to play for. Raikkonen was still in the hunt, but only just, as he was now 17 points down.

A lap from the end, Heidfeld pulled off from sixth. Then, as a delighted Coulthard finished fourth and Fisichella fifth, Kubica and Massa had a fierce battle for sixth, with Massa passing at the final corner. The final point looked to have gone to Liuzzi, but he was given a 25s penalty for passing Sutil under yellow flags, promoting Sutil to eighth.

FUJI SPEEDWAY ROUND 15

Date: **30 September 2007** Laps: **67** Distance: **191.084 miles/ 307.520km** Weather: **Cool, foggy and very wet**

RACE RESULT

Position	Driver	Team	Result	Stops	Qualifying Time	Grid
1	Lewis Hamilton	McLaren	2h00m34.579s	1	1m25.638s	1
2	Heikki Kovalainen	Renault	2h00m42.956s	1	1m26.232s	11
3	Kimi Räikkönen	Ferrari	2h00m44.057s	3	1m25.516s	3
4	David Coulthard	Red Bull	2h00m54.876s	1	1m26.247s	12
5	Giancarlo Fisichella	Renault	2h01m13.443s	1	1m26.033s	10
6	Felipe Massa	Ferrari	2h01m23.621s	4	1m25.765s	4
7	Robert Kubica	BMW Sauber	2h01m23.864s	2	1m27.225s	9
8	Adrian Sutil	Spyker	2h01m34.708s	1	1m28.628s	20
9	Vitantonio Liuzzi	Toro Rosso	2h01m55.201s*	2	1m26.948s	14**
10	Rubens Barrichello	Honda	2h02m02.921s	2	1m27.323s	17
11	Jenson Button	Honda	66 laps/suspension	1	1m26.913s	6
12	Sakon Yamamoto	Spyker	66 laps	2	1m29.668s	22
13	Jarno Trulli	Toyota	66 laps	2	1m26.253s	13
14	Nick Heidfeld	BMW Sauber	65 laps/electronics	1	1m26.505s	5
15	Takuma Sato	Super Aguri	65 laps/puncture	2	1m28.792s	21
R	Ralf Schumacher	Toyota	55 laps/puncture	3	no time	15
R	Anthony Davidson	Super Aguri	54 laps/throttle sensor	1	1m27.564s	19
R	Nico Rosberg	Williams	49 laps/electronics	2	1m26.728s	16***
R	Sebastian Vettel	Toro Rosso	46 laps/crash damage	1	1m26.973s	8
R	Mark Webber	Red Bull	45 laps/accident	1	1m26.914s	7
R	Fernando Alonso	McLaren	41 laps/accident	1	1m25.438s	2
R	Alexander Wurz	Williams	19 laps/accident	1	1m27.454s	18

FASTEST LAP: HAMILTON, 1M28.193S (114.059MPH/186.259KPH) ON LAP 27
RACE LEADERS: HAMILTON, 1-28, 41-6; VETTEL, 29-31; WEBBER, 32-36; KOVALAINEN, 37-39; FISICHELLA, 40
* INCLUDING 25s PENALTY FOR OVERTAKING UNDER YELLOW FLAGS ** STARTED FROM THE PITLANE *** DENOTES 10-PLACE GRID PENALTY

TALKING POINT: MISDEMEANOURS IN THE MIST

Toro Rosso's rookie Sebastian Vettel was lambasted after retiring from the Japanese GP as he had not only blown his chance of third place, but also taken out Mark Webber. Yes, he'd taken a chunk out of Red Bull's double ambitions. Webber blamed the German's inexperience and the officials gave him a 10-place grid penalty for the following race. This was later overturned – only for Sebastian to pick up a five-place penalty for impeding a driver in qualifying – but Lewis Hamilton was summoned in China as he had been accused of taking a strange line behind the safety car that caused those behind to slow and might have triggered the incident in his wake.

A loss of attention or perhaps something else led to Vettel knocking Webber out of second place.

CHINESE GP

This should have been the race at which Lewis Hamilton was crowned world champion, but a slip into a gravel trap at pit entrance as he came in for a pit stop left his McLaren stranded and allowed his rivals Alonso and Raikkonen to close in.

For Lewis Hamilton, this ought to have been the grand prix at which his dreams came true. The massive facilities of the ultra-modern Shanghai International Circuit should have been the backdrop to a careful run to a healthy helping of points that would leave him either crowned as the first ever rookie world champion or heading to the final race in Brazil with a shoo-in for the crown.

As it was, Hamilton trailed Alonso and Ferrari's duo through practice and much of qualifying. Then, as if to add another twist to the title battle, and especially to his intra-team scrap with Alonso, he lined everything up on his final flier and delivered, not only taking pole position, but lapping fully 0.66s faster than his team-mate. Alonso, who had been out with the same fuel load, was humiliated to the extent that he kicked in a door in the McLaren paddock HQ. The Spaniard would start fourth, behind the Ferraris of Kimi Raikkonen and Felipe Massa.

Before the start, it was hard to guess what the weather would do, but the sky was leaden and the humidity soaring. Rain was due, but when? All started on intermediate tyres, though, and the rain hit just after the start. Not that this worried Hamilton as he had made a perfect start and was easily clear of Raikkonen by the time he reached Turn 1.

Massa didn't have the same luxury, as Alonso forced his way into third out of Turn 2, only to lose traction out of Turn 3 and thus lose it again at the Turn 6 hairpin as the Ferrari driver dived up his inside.

Behind them, David Coulthard made the most of qualifying fifth for Red Bull by holding down this position, but Ralf Schumacher spun out of sixth at Turn 1, while Jenson Button lost ground and Vitantonio Liuzzi went in the opposite direction up to seventh.

As rain arrived, Hamilton was 1.5s up after two laps and 6.6s clear after 10. The big question as track conditions changed was how much fuel Hamilton was carrying, as the ease with which he was pulling clear suggested that he'd be the first of the quartet to pit. And so he was, on lap 15, when he was 8.6s clear of Raikkonen. Such was his early-race speed, that Hamilton was able to rejoin fourth, still just ahead of Coulthard. Interestingly, no new tyres were taken on.

This proved to be the popular choice with most pit callers, and TV commentator Martin Brundle voiced concern that tyre wear could prove a factor. How right he was to be.

Massa pitted two laps later, then Raikkonen and Alonso on lap 18. Hamilton was to remain in front, but his advantage over Raikkonen had been halved.

What followed emphasised how conditions were changing as Alexander Wurz was lapping faster than anyone, having been the first to change onto dry tyres. Yet, no sooner did this begin to look to be the correct decision than rain returned. So the teams' weather experts resumed their research.

What was clear, was that Hamilton was struggling for grip and Raikkonen was onto his tail by lap 27. Hamilton could have let him go, as he didn't need to win, but he fought

A win for Raikkonen kept him in with a chance of catching Hamilton for the world title.

until he slid wide on lap 29 and Raikkonen was into the lead in a flash.

Two laps later, with canvas showing through his left rear tyre, Hamilton was called in to the pits, but he never made it, sliding into a gravel trap at pit entry. It was agonising as he tried to drive through it, but the car bogged down and he was out. Quite simply, McLaren had waited one lap too long and had paid the price.

So, the race was Raikkonen's and Alonso was safe in second, a finishing order that would move Alonso to within four points and Raikkonen to within seven, meaning that the title battle would go to the final round.

While all this was happening, Robert Kubica took the lead when the first three pitted the lap after Hamilton's faux pas, but his joy and inspired decision to go onto dry tyres on lap 25 came to naught when his BMW Sauber's hydraulics failed. So Raikkonen assumed control ahead of Alonso.

Third place at this stage was held not by Massa but by Toro Rosso's Sebastian Vettel who had been put back to 17th on the grid. The one-stopping rookie held on to within 10 laps of the finish when Massa claimed the final podium position back. Toro Rosso's great day was made better still when Vettel's team-mate Liuzzi finished sixth behind Button but ahead of Nick Heidfeld.

SHANGHAI ROUND 16
Date: **7 October 2007** Laps: **56** Distance: **189.680 miles/305.250km**
Weather: **Warm and wet then drying**

RACE RESULT

Position	Driver	Team	Result	Stops	Qualifying Time	Grid
1	**Kimi Räikkönen**	Ferrari	1h37m58.395s	2	1m36.044s	2
2	**Fernando Alonso**	McLaren	1h38m08.201s	2	1m36.576s	4
3	**Felipe Massa**	Ferrari	1h38m11.286s	2	1m36.221s	3
4	**Sebastian Vettel**	Toro Rosso	1h38m51.904s	1	1m36.891s	17*
5	**Jenson Button**	Honda	1h39m07.061s	2	1m39.285s	10
6	**Vitantonio Liuzzi**	Toro Rosso	1h39m12.068s	2	1m36.862s	12
7	**Nick Heidfeld**	BMW Sauber	1h39m12.619s	2	1m38.455s	8
8	**David Coulthard**	Red Bull	1h39m19.145s	2	1m37.619s	5
9	**Heikki Kovalainen**	Renault	1h39m19.581s	1	1m36.991s	13
10	**Mark Webber**	Red Bull	1h39m23.080s	3	1m38.153s	7
11	**Giancarlo Fisichella**	Renault	1h39m25.078s	2	1m37.290s	18
12	**Alexander Wurz**	Williams	55 laps	2	1m37.456s	19
13	**Jarno Trulli**	Toyota	55 laps	1	1m36.959s	12
14	**Takuma Sato**	Super Aguri	55 laps	1	1m38.218s	20
15	**Rubens Barrichello**	Honda	55 laps	3	1m37.215s	16
16	**Nico Rosberg**	Williams	54 laps	3	1m37.483s	15
17	**Sakon Yamamoto**	Spyker	53 laps	4	1m39.336s	22
R	**Robert Kubica**	BMW Sauber	33 laps/hydraulics	1	1m38.472s	9
R	**Lewis Hamilton**	McLaren	30 laps/spun off	1	1m35.908s	1
R	**Ralf Schumacher**	Toyota	25 laps/spun off	1	1m38.013s	6
R	**Adrian Sutil**	Spyker	24 laps/accident	2	1m38.668s	21
R	**Anthony Davidson**	Super Aguri	11 laps/brakes	1	1m37.247s	14

FASTEST LAP: MASSA, 1M37.454S, 125.120MPH/201.362KPH ON LAP 56
RACE LEADERS: HAMILTON 1-15, 20-28; RAIKKONEN, 16-19, 29-32, 34-56; KUBICA 33
* DENOTES MOVED BACK FIVE PLACES FOR IMPEDING ANOTHER DRIVER IN QUALIFYING

TALKING POINT: McLAREN TAKES THE HEAT OFF HAMILTON

You could feel the pain on McLaren's pit wall when they saw the images of Lewis Hamilton running into the gravel at pit entry and failing to carry enough momentum to drive out. ITV commentator Martin Brundle had already suggested that it was time for Hamilton to pit as he could do nothing to resist Raikkonen. Brundle reckoned that the left rear tyre was worn to the canvas. Hamilton had to come in. The team took the blame, CEO Martin Whitmarsh saying: "With hindsight, we left him out a lap too long and his tyres were pretty worn. The weather was changeable and we wanted to make sure that we weren't taking any risks."

With his tyres all but bald, Lewis Hamilton slipped off the track coming into the pit lane, scoring zero.

BRAZILIAN GP

The world title was there to win and there to lose. For British fans, it was disappointment as McLaren and Lewis Hamilton grabbed the latter option, leaving it clear for Kimi Raikkonen to become world champion at last.

Ferraris to the fore as Felipe Massa leading Kimi Raikkonen and Lewis Hamilton, just before the shape of the race was decided by the Finn.

One look at the respective points tallies for Lewis Hamilton, his McLaren team-mate Fernando Alonso and Kimi Raikkonen made it clear that Hamilton had a clear advantage. For, despite his disastrous Chinese GP, he was still four points clear of Alonso and seven ahead of the Ferrari ace.

Pole position was grabbed by Felipe Massa in the other Ferrari. He would be expected to help Raikkonen where possible. Knowing that it was victory or nothing, Raikkonen would have loved to be next, but a stunning lap from Hamilton left him second. If that was bad for Raikkonen. Alonso would start fourth.

Hamilton had to keep Alonso in sight, but he was beaten off the line by Raikkonen, who even had a look at passing Massa. This would

have been around the outside, so he tucked back in behind Massa out of Turn 1 and tripped up in avoidance, causing Hamilton to lift and lose momentum on the drop to the Senna S. In a flash, Alonso used his extra speed to go inside him and claim third place. This was not a disaster, but Hamilton let his racer's instincts take hold and tried to get the place back at Turn 4, locked up and ran wide. Mark Webber, Robert Kubica, Nick Heidfeld and Jarno Trulli went past before he rejoined.

Seven laps later, Turn 4 was again where it happened, with his engine dropping into neutral for 30 agonising seconds until, with the help of his engineer over the radio, he managed to trigger the fire-up sequence and get motive power back. This left him 18th.

By this stage, Alonso simply couldn't match the Ferraris' pace and all guessed that Massa would cede the lead to Raikkonen when required, so the title would be the Finn's and not his, by a single point.

This was without considering a recovery drive from Hamilton, but even though he was picking up the odd position, he would have to have a miracle to come back into contention.

The first bit of help for Hamilton came on lap 15 when Webber's year was brought to an end with another mechanical failure.

Lapping at the same speed as the Ferraris, Hamilton climbed to 11th, which became 10th when Jenson Button retired, when Massa became the first frontrunner to pit on lap 20.

Being so far behind, McLaren took a

gamble with Hamilton. None of the teams were optimistic about the longevity of strong performance from the softer tyres, which they all had to fit for one race stint, but it was decided to send Hamilton out for a short second stint on these and short-fuel his car accordingly. This would have been a masterstroke, but the team looked at the tyres on which he'd just done 22 laps and realised that they were so worn that his harder set for the planned third stint would never last the 35 laps required. So, a third pit stop would be necessary and that wiped out any hope he had of making it up to the fifth place he required to become champion.

Massa continued to lead, but Raikkonen had been fuelled for a longer stint and would make his second stop three laps later and emerge in the lead, just, confirming that fifth is Hamilton's target. As he's running eighth, this seems unlikely, and his best hope after Jarno Trulli gives him a place by making his third stop is for Rosberg to clash with the BMW Saubers, which looks likely until he drops them. So, it's all over and Raikkonen takes the win to become a surprising but deserved champion. Alonso was a distant third, neutered by the Ferraris' pace, and Rosberg an excellent fourth.

The Williams and BMW Sauber point finishers were later given a scare, see below.

INTERLAGOS ROUND 17
Date: 21 October 2007 Laps: 71 Distance: 190.083 miles/305.909km
Weather: **Sunny and hot**

RACE RESULT

Position	Driver	Team	Result	Stops	Qualifying Time	Grid
1	Kimi Räikkönen	Ferrari	1h28m15.270s	2	1m12.322s	3
2	Felipe Massa	Ferrari	1h28m16.763s	2	1m11.931s	1
3	Fernando Alonso	McLaren	1h29m12.289s	2	1m12.356s	4
4	Nico Rosberg	Williams	1h29m18.118s	2	1m13.477s	10
5	Robert Kubica	BMW Sauber	1h29m26.227s	3	1m13.129s	7
6	Nick Heidfeld	BMW Sauber	1h29m26.587s	2	1m13.081s	6
7	Lewis Hamilton	McLaren	70 laps	3	1m12.082s	2
8	Jarno Trulli	Toyota	70 laps	3	1m13.195s	8
9	David Coulthard	Red Bull	70 laps	2	1m13.272s	9
10	Kazuki Nakajima	Williams	70 laps	2	1m14.417s	19
11	Ralf Schumacher	Toyota	70 laps	2	1m13.315s	15
12	Takuma Sato	Super Aguri	69 laps	2	1m14.098s	18
13	Vitantonio Liuzzi	Toro Rosso	69 laps	3	1m13.251s	14
14	Anthony Davidson	Super Aguri	68 laps	3	1m14.596s	20
R	Adrian Sutil	Spyker	43 laps/brakes	5	1m15.217s	21*
R	Rubens Barrichello	Honda	40 laps/engine	2	1m12.932s	11
R	Heikki Kovalainen	Renault	35 laps/accident	1	1m14.078s	17
R	Sebastian Vettel	Toro Rosso	34 laps/hydraulics	1	1m13.058s	13
R	Jenson Button	Honda	20 laps/engine	0	1m13.469s	16
R	Mark Webber	Red Bull	14 laps/transmission	0	1m12.928s	5
R	Sakon Yamamoto	Spyker	2 laps/accident	0	1m15.487s	22
R	Giancarlo Fisichella	Renault	2 laps/accident	0	1m12.968s	12

FASTEST LAP: RAIKKONEN, 1M12.445S, 133.051MPH/214.125KPH ON LAP 66
RACE LEADERS: MASSA 1-19, 23-49; RAIKKONEN, 20-21, 50-71; ALONSO 22
* DENOTES STARTED THE RACE FROM THE PITLANE

TALKING POINT: WHEN BREAKING THE RULES IS NOT ILLEGAL

The journalists had scrapped their features on Hamilton becoming the first rookie champion and lauded Raikkonen's 11th hour advance. But as darkness fell, a spanner was thrown into the works: the cars that had finished fourth to sixth were under investigation. The problem was that the fuel in both Williams and BMW Saubers was found to have been too cool, that's to say more than 10 degrees below the ambient temperature, when measured during their pit stops, thus offering the teams the advantage of being able to fit more into the cars. No action was taken, so McLaren appealed, as "a matter of principle". They were later cleared.

The Williams and BMW Sauber finishers were locked up after there was found to have been an irregularity.

Considered as having only a mathematical chance of overtaking the McLaren drivers to become world champion in the Brazilian finale, Kimi Raikkonen maintained his strong end of season form and harvested everything that Lewis Hamilton's misfortune offered him to take a world title that many felt he had deserved for years. Of course, ever cool Kimi said that everything was under control.

FINAL RESULTS 2007

	DRIVER	NAT.		ENGINE	R1	R2	R3	R4
1.	KIMI RAIKKONEN	FIN		FERRARI F2007	1PF	3	5	R
2.	LEWIS HAMILTON	GBR		McLAREN-MERCEDES MP4-22	3	2F	2	2
3.	FERNANDO ALONSO	SPA		McLAREN-MERCEDES MP4-22	2	1	3	3
4.	FELIPE MASSA	BRA		FERRARI F2007	6	5P	1PF	1PF
5.	NICK HEIDFELD	GER		BMW SAUBER F1.07	4	4	4	R
6.	ROBERT KUBICA	POL		BMW SAUBER F1.07	R	18	6	4
7.	HEIKKI KOVALAINEN	FIN		RENAULT R27	10	8	9	7
8.	GIANCARLO FISICHELLA	ITA		RENAULT R27	5	6	8	9
9.	NICO ROSBERG	GER		WILLIAMS-TOYOTA FW29	7	R	10	6
10.	DAVID COULTHARD	GBR		RED BULL-RENAULT RB3	R	R	R	5
11.	ALEXANDER WURZ	AUT		WILLIAMS-TOYOTA FW29	R	9	11	R
12.	MARK WEBBER	AUS		RED BULL-RENAULT RB3	13	10	R	R
13.	JARNO TRULLI	ITA		TOYOTA TF107	9	7	7	R
14.	SEBASTIAN VETTEL	GER		BMW SAUBER F1.07	-	-	-	-
				TORO ROSSO-FERRARI STR2	-	-	-	-
15.	JENSON BUTTON	GBR		HONDA RA107	15	12	R	12
16.	RALF SCHUMACHER	GER		TOYOTA TF107	8	15	12	R
17.	TAKUMA SATO	JAP		SUPER AGURI-HONDA SA06	12	13	R	8
18.	VITANTONIO LIUZZI	ITA		TORO ROSSO-FERRARI STR2	14	17	R	R
19.	ADRIAN SUTIL	GER		SPYKER-FERRARI F8-VII	17	R	15	13
	RUBENS BARRICHELLO	BRA		HONDA RA107	11	11	13	10
	SCOTT SPEED	USA		TORO ROSSO-FERRARI STR2	R	14	R	R
	KAZUKI NAKAJIMA	JAP		WILLIAMS-TOYOTA FW29	-	-	-	-
	ANTHONY DAVIDSON	GBR		SUPER AGURI-HONDA SA07	16	16	R	11
	SAKON YAMAMOTO	JAP		SPYKER-FERRARI F8-VII	-	-	-	-
	CHRISTIJAN ALBERS	NED		SPYKER-FERRARI F8-VII	R	R	14	14
	MARKUS WINKELHOCK	GER		SPYKER-FERRARI F8-VII	-	-	-	-

SCORING

1st	10 points
2nd	8 points
3rd	6 points
4th	5 points
5th	4 points
6th	3 points
7th	2 points
8th	1 point

(RACE RESULTS FOR BOTH DRIVERS, ie. FIRST AND SECOND LISTED AS 1/2, WITH THE TEAM'S BETTER RESULT LISTED FIRST)

		R1	R2	R3	R4
1.	FERRARI	1/6	3/5	1/5	1/R
2.	BMW SAUBER	4/R	4/18	4/6	4/R
3.	RENAULT	5/10	6/8	8/9	7/9
4.	WILLIAMS-TOYOTA	7/R	9/R	10/11	6/R
5.	RED BULL-RENAULT	13/R	10/R	R/R	5/R
6.	TOYOTA	8/9	7/15	7/12	R/R
7.	TORO ROSSO-FERRARI	14/R	14/17	R/R	R/R
8.	HONDA	11/15	11/12	13/R	10/12
9.	SUPER AGURI-HONDA	12/16	13/16	R/R	8/11
10.	SPYKER-FERRARI	17/R	R/R	14/15	13/14
11.	McLAREN-MERCEDES	2/3	1/2	2/3	2/3

SYMBOLS AND GRAND PRIX KEY

D DISQUALIFIED   **F** FASTEST LAP   **NC** NOT CLASSIFIED   **NS** NON-STARTER   **P** POLE POSITION   **R** RETIRED   **W** WITHDREW

R5	R6	R7	R8	R9	R10	R11	R12	R13	R14	R15	R16	R17	TOTAL POINTS
8	5	4F	1	1F	RP	2F	2F	3	1P	3	1	1F	110
2	1P	1P	3	3P	9	1P	5	2	4	1PF	RP	7	109
1PF	7F	2	7	2	1	4	3	1PF	3	R	2	3	109
3	D	3	2PF	5	2F	13	1P	R	2F	6	3F	2P	94
6	2	R	5	6	6	3	4	4	5	14	7	6	61
5	R	-	4	4	7	5	8	5	9	7	R	5	39
13	4	5	15	7	8	8	6	7	8	2	9	R	30
4	D	9	6	8	10	12	9	12	R	5	11	R	21
12	10	16	9	12	R	7	7	6	6	R	16	4	20
14	R	R	13	11	5	11	10	R	R	4	8	9	14
7	3	10	14	13	4	14	11	13	R	R	12	-	13
R	9	7	12	R	3	9	R	9	7	R	10	R	10
15	R	6	R	R	13	10	16	11	11	13	13	8	8
-	-	8	-	-	-	-	-	-	-	-	-	-	
-	-	-	-	-	16	19	18	R	R	4	R		6
11	R	12	8	10	R	R	13	8	R	11	5	R	6
16	8	R	10	R	R	6	12	15	10	R	R	11	5
17	6	R	16	14	R	15	18	16	15	15	14	12	4
R	R	17	R	16	R	R	15	17	12	9	6	13	3
R	R	14	17	R	R	17	21	19	14	8	R	R	1
10	12	R	11	9	11	18	17	10	13	10	15	R	0
9	R	13	R	R	R	-	-	-	-	-	-	-	0
-	-	-	-	-	-	-	-	-	-	-	-	10	0
18	11	11	R	R	12	R	14	14	16	R	R	14	0
-	-	-	-	-	-	R	20	20	17	12	17	R	0
19	R	15	R	15	-	-	-	-	-	-	-	-	0
-	-	-	-	-	R	-	-	-	-	-	-	-	0

R5	R6	R7	R8	R9	R10	R11	R12	R13	R14	R15	R16	R17	
3/8	5/D	3/4	1/2	1/5	2/R	2/13	1/2	3/R	1/2	3/6	1/3	1/2	204
5/6	2/R	8/R	4/5	4/6	6/7	3/5	4/8	4/5	5/9	7/14	7/R	5/6	101
4/13	4/D	5/9	6/15	7/8	8/10	8/12	6/9	7/12	8/R	2/5	9/11	R/R	51
7/12	3/10	10/16	9/14	12/13	4/R	7/14	7/11	6/13	6/R	R/R	12/16	4/10	33
14/R	9/R	7/R	12/13	11/R	3/5	9/11	10/R	9/R	7/R	4/R	8/10	9/R	24
15/16	8/R	6/R	10/R	R/R	13/R	6/10	12/16	11/15	10/11	13/R	13/R	8/11	13
9/R	R/R	13/17	R/R	16/R	R/R	16/R	15/19	17/18	12/R	9/R	4/6	13/R	8
10/11	12/R	12/R	8/11	9/10	11/R	18/R	13/17	8/10	13/R	10/R	5/15	R/R	6
17/18	6/11	11/R	16/R	14/R	12/R	15/R	14/18	14/16	15/16	15/R	14/R	12/14	4
19/R	R/R	14/15	17/R	15/R	R/R	17/R	20/21	19/20	14/17	8/12	R/17	R/R	1
1/2	1/7	1/2	3/7	2/3	1/9	1/4	3/5	1/2	3/4	1/R	2/R	3/7	0*

* McLaren was excluded from the constructors' championship for one of its employees being found in possession of Ferrari documents

FORMULA 1 RECORDS

MOST GRANDS PRIX STARTS

DRIVERS

256	Riccardo Patrese	(ITA)	171	Niki Lauda	(AUT)	135	Jean-Pierre Jarier	(FRA)
252	Rubens Barrichello	(BRA)	165	Jacques Villeneuve	(CDN)	134	Nick Heidfeld	(GER)
250	Michael Schumacher	(GER)	163	Thierry Boutsen	(BEL)	132	Eddie Cheever	(USA)
229	David Coulthard	(GBR)	162	Mika Hakkinen	(FIN)		Clay Regazzoni	(SUI)
210	Gerhard Berger	(AUT)		Johnny Herbert	(GBR)	128	Mario Andretti	(USA)
208	Andrea de Cesaris	(ITA)	161	Ayrton Senna	(BRA)	126	Jack Brabham	(AUS)
204	Nelson Piquet	(BRA)	159	Heinz-Harald Frentzen	(GER)	123	Ronnie Peterson	(SWE)
201	Jean Alesi	FRA)	158	Martin Brundle	(GBR)	122	Kimi Raikkonen	(FIN)
199	Alain Prost	(FRA)		Olivier Panis	(FRA)	119	Pierluigi Martini	(ITA)
196	Giancarlo Fisichella	(ITA)	152	John Watson	(GBR)	116	Damon Hill	(GBR)
194	Michele Alboreto	(ITA)	149	Rene Arnoux	(FRA)		Jacky Ickx	(BEL)
187	Nigel Mansell	(GBR)	147	Eddie Irvine	(GBR)		Alan Jones	(AUS)
184	Jarno Trulli	(ITA)		Derek Warwick	(GBR)	114	Keke Rosberg	(FIN)
180	Ralf Schumacher	(GER)	146	Carlos Reutemann	(ARG)		Patrick Tambay	(FRA)
176	Graham Hill	(GBR)	144	Emerson Fittipaldi	(BRA)	112	Denny Hulme	(NZL)
175	Jacques Laffite	(FRA)	136	Jenson Button	(GBR)		Jody Scheckter	(RSA)

CONSTRUCTORS

741	Ferrari	383	Arrows	197	BRM	
631	McLaren	376	Toro Rosso (nee Minardi)	188	Red Bull (nee Stewart then	
550	Williams	317	Benetton		Jaguar Racing)	
490	Lotus	285	Spyker (nee Jordan then Midland)	153	Honda Racing (nee BAR)	
418	Tyrrell	252	BMW Sauber	132	Osella	
409	Prost	230	March	129	Cooper	
394	Brabham	228	Renault	126	Larrousse	

Rubens Barrichello, shown in his first season of Formula One with Jordan in 1993, is to become the driver with the most grand prix starts to his name.

Nigel Mansell was able to dominate 1992 for Williams like few have ever managed before or since, winning nine of the season's 16 grands prix.

MOST GRANDS PRIX WINS

DRIVERS

91	Michael Schumacher	(GER)	14	Jack Brabham	(AUS)	8	Denny Hulme	(NZL)		
51	Alain Prost	(FRA)		Emerson Fittipaldi	(BRA)		Jacky Ickx	(BEL)		
41	Ayrton Senna	(BRA)		Graham Hill	(GBR)	7	Rene Arnoux	(FRA)		
31	Nigel Mansell	(GBR)	13	Alberto Ascari	(ITA)		Juan Pablo Montoya	(COL)		
27	Jackie Stewart	(GBR)		David Coulthard	(GBR)	6	Tony Brooks	(GBR)		
25	Jim Clark	(GBR)	12	Mario Andretti	(USA)		Jacques Laffite	(FRA)		
	Niki Lauda	(AUT)		Alan Jones	(AUS)		Riccardo Patrese	(FRA)		
24	Juan Manuel Fangio	(ARG)		Carlos Reutemann	(ARG)		Jochen Rindt	(AUT)		
23	Nelson Piquet	(BRA)	11	Jacques Villeneuve	(CDN)		Ralf Schumacher	(GER)		
22	Damon Hill	(GBR)	10	Gerhard Berger	(AUT)		John Surtees	(GBR)		
20	Mika Hakkinen	(FIN)		James Hunt	(GBR)		Gilles Villeneuve	(CDN)		
19	Fernando Alonso	(SPA)		Ronnie Peterson	(SWE)					
16	Stirling Moss	(GBR)		Jody Scheckter	(RSA)					
15	Kimi Raikkonen	(FIN)	9	Rubens Barrichello	(BRA)					

CONSTRUCTORS

201	Ferrari	10	Alfa Romeo	1	Eagle	
156	McLaren	9	Ligier		Hesketh	
113	Williams		Maserati		Honda Racing (nee BAR)	
79	Lotus		Matra		Penske	
35	Brabham		Mercedes		Porsche	
33	Renault		Vanwall		Shadow	
27	Benetton	4	Spyker (nee Jordan then Midland)		Red Bull (nee Stewart then	
23	Tyrrell	3	March		Jaguar Racing)	
17	BRM		Wolf			
16	Cooper	2	Honda			

LEFT: Michael Schumacher sends his home crowd wild by winning the German GP at Hockenheim for Ferrari in 2004.
RIGHT: Jim Clark raced to five wins in a row in 1965. This is at Clermont-Ferrand.
BELOW RIGHT: Andrea de Cesaris, shown racing for Alfa Romeo in 1982, remains the driver with the worst starts-to-wins ratio.

MOST GRANDS PRIX WINS IN ONE SEASON

DRIVERS

13	Michael Schumacher	(GER)	2004		Fernando Alonso	(SPA)	2006		Juan Manuel Fangio	(ARG)	1954
11	Michael Schumacher	(GER)	2002		Jim Clark	(GBR)	1963		Damon Hill	(GBR)	1994
9	Nigel Mansell	(GBR)	1992		Alain Prost	(FRA)	1984		James Hunt	(GBR)	1976
	Michael Schumacher	(GER)	1995		Alain Prost	(FRA)	1988		Nigel Mansell	(GBR)	1987
	Michael Schumacher	(GER)	2000		Alain Prost	(FRA)	1993		Kimi Raikkonen	(FIN)	2007
	Michael Schumacher	(GER)	2001		Kimi Raikkonen	(FIN)	2005		Michael Schumacher	(GER)	1998
8	Mika Hakkinen	(FIN)	1998		Ayrton Senna	(BRA)	1991		Michael Schumacher	(GER)	2003
	Damon Hill	(GBR)	1996		Jacques Villeneuve	(CDN)	1997		Michael Schumacher	(GER)	2006
	Michael Schumacher	(GER)	1994	6	Mario Andretti	(USA)	1978		Ayrton Senna	(BRA)	1989
	Ayrton Senna	(BRA)	1988		Alberto Ascari	(ITA)	1952		Ayrton Senna	(BRA)	1990
7	Fernando Alonso	(SPA)	2005		Jim Clark	(GBR)	1965				

CONSTRUCTORS

15	Ferrari	2004		Ferrari	2007		Ferrari	1953		Ferrari	1979
	Ferrari	2002		McLaren	1998		Lotus	1963		Ferrari	1990
	McLaren	1988		Williams	1986		Lotus	1973		Ferrari	1996
12	McLaren	1984		Williams	1987		McLaren	1999		Ferrari	1998
	Williams	1996	8	Benetton	1994		McLaren	2000		Ferrari	1999
11	Benetton	1995		Ferrari	2003		Tyrrell	1971		Lotus	1965
10	Ferrari	2000		Lotus	1978		Williams	1991		Lotus	1970
	McLaren	2005		McLaren	1991		Williams	1994		Matra	1969
	McLaren	1989		McLaren	2007	6	Alfa Romeo	1950		McLaren	1976
	Williams	1992		Renault	2005		Alfa Romeo	1951		McLaren	1985
	Williams	1993		Renault	2006		Cooper	1960		McLaren	1990
9	Ferrari	2001		Williams	1997		Ferrari	1975		Vanwall	1958
	Ferrari	2006	7	Ferrari	1952		Ferrari	1976		Williams	1980

MOST CONSECUTIVE WINS

9	Alberto Ascari	(ITA)	1952/53
7	Michael Schumacher	(GER)	2004
6	Michael Schumacher	(GER)	2000/01
5	Jack Brabham	(AUS)	1960
	Jim Clark	(GBR)	1965
	Nigel Mansell	(GBR)	1992
	Michael Schumacher	(GER)	2004
4	Fernando Alonso	(SPA)	2006
	Jack Brabham	(AUS)	1966
	Jim Clark	(GBR)	1963
	Juan Manuel Fangio	(ARG)	1953/54
	Damon Hill	(GBR)	1995/96
	Alain Prost	(FRA)	1993
	Jochen Rindt	(AUT)	1970
	Michael Schumacher	(GER)	1994
	Michael Schumacher	(GER)	2002
	Ayrton Senna	(BRA)	1988
	Ayrton Senna	(BRA)	1991

GRANDS PRIX STARTS WITHOUT A WIN

208	Andrea de Cesaris	(ITA)	119	Pierluigi Martini	(ITA)	97	Chris Amon	(NZL)
158	Martin Brundle	(GBR)	111	Mika Salo	(FIN)	95	Ukyo Katayama	(JAP)
147	Derek Warwick	(GBR)	109	Philippe Alliot	(FRA)	93	Ivan Capelli	(ITA)
135	Jean-Pierre Jarier	(FRA)	107	Jos Verstappen	(NED)	89	Takuma Sato	(JAP)
134	Nick Heidfeld	(GER)	104	Mark Webber	(AUS)	84	Jonathan Palmer	(GBR)
132	Eddie Cheever	(USA)	99	Pedro Diniz	(BRA)	82	Marc Surer	(SUI)

MOST POLE POSITIONS

DRIVERS

68	Michael Schumacher	(GER)
65	Ayrton Senna	(BRA)
33	Jim Clark	(GBR)
	Alain Prost	(FRA)
32	Nigel Mansell	(GBR)
29	Juan Manuel Fangio	(ARG)
26	Mika Hakkinen	(FIN)
24	Niki Lauda	(AUT)
	Nelson Piquet	(BRA)
20	Damon Hill	(GBR)
18	Mario Andretti	(USA)
	Rene Arnoux	(FRA)
17	Jackie Stewart	(GBR)
16	Fernando Alonso	(SPA)
	Stirling Moss	(GBR)
14	Alberto Ascari	(ITA)
	James Hunt	(GBR)
	Ronnie Peterson	(SWE)
	Kimi Raikkonen	(FIN)
13	Rubens Barrichello	(BRA)
	Jack Brabham	(AUS)
	Graham Hill	(GBR)
	Jacky Ickx	(BEL)
	Juan Pablo Montoya	(COL)
	Jacques Villeneuve	(CDN)
12	Gerhard Berger	(AUT)
	David Coulthard	(GBR)
10	Jochen Rindt	(AUT)
9	Felipe Massa	(BRA)
8	Riccardo Patrese	(ITA)
	John Surtees	(GBR)

CONSTRUCTORS

195	Ferrari
133	McLaren
125	Williams
107	Lotus
50	Renault
39	Brabham
16	Benetton
14	Tyrrell
12	Alfa Romeo
11	BRM
	Cooper
10	Maserati
9	Prost
8	Mercedes
7	Vanwall
5	March
4	Matra
3	Honda Racing (nee BAR)
	Shadow
2	Spyker (nee Jordan then Midland)
	Lancia
	Toyota
1	Red Bull (nee Stewart then Jaguar Racing)

BELOW: Ayrton Senna was long the king of pole positions, particularly for McLaren, until Michael Schumacher overhauled his tally, albeit from many more starts.

MOST POLE POSITIONS IN ONE SEASON

DRIVERS

14	Nigel Mansell	(GBR)	1992		Damon Hill	(GBR)	1996			Michael Schumacher	(GER)	2004
13	Alain Prost	(FRA)	1993		Niki Lauda	(AUT)	1974			Ayrton Senna	(BRA)	1986
	Ayrton Senna	(BRA)	1988		Niki Lauda	(AUT)	1975			Ayrton Senna	(BRA)	1991
	Ayrton Senna	(BRA)	1989		Ronnie Peterson	(SWE)	1973	7		Mario Andretti	(USA)	1977
11	Mika Hakkinen	(FIN)	1999		Nelson Piquet	(BRA)	1984			Jim Clark	(GBR)	1963
	Michael Schumacher	(GER)	2001		Michael Schumacher	(GER)	2000			Damon Hill	(GBR)	1995
10	Ayrton Senna	(BRA)	1990	8	Mario Andretti	(USA)	1978			Juan Pablo Montoya	(COL)	2002
	Jacques Villeneuve	(CDN)	1997		James Hunt	(GBR)	1976			Michael Schumacher	(GER)	2002
9	Mika Hakkinen	(FIN)	1998		Nigel Mansell	(GBR)	1987			Ayrton Senna	(BRA)	1985

CONSTRUCTORS

15	McLaren	1988		Williams	1996	9	Brabham	1984
	McLaren	1989	11	Ferrari	2001		Ferrari	1975
	Williams	1992		McLaren	1999		Ferrari	2007
	Williams	1993		Williams	1997			
12	Ferrari	2004	10	Ferrari	1974			
	Lotus	1978		Ferrari	2000			
	McLaren	1990		Ferrari	2002			
	McLaren	1998		Lotus	1973			
	Williams	1987		McLaren	1991			
	Williams	1995		Renault	1982			

ABOVE: Damon Hill leads Williams team-mate Alain Prost in the Canadian GP in 1993, with Gerhard Berger and Jean Alesi in their wake. Prost would be champion that year.

MOST FASTEST LAPS

DRIVERS

75	Michael Schumacher	(GER)	21	Gerhard Berger	(AUT)	13	Alberto Ascari	(ITA)
41	Alain Prost	(FRA)	19	Damon Hill	(GBR)		Alan Jones	(AUS)
30	Nigel Mansell	(GBR)		Stirling Moss	(GBR)		Riccardo Patrese	(ITA)
28	Jim Clark	(GBR)		Ayrton Senna	(BRA)	12	Rene Arnoux	(FRA)
25	Mika Hakkinen	(FIN)	18	David Coulthard	(GBR)		Jack Brabham	(AUS)
	Kimi Raikkonen	(FIN)	15	Rubens Barrichello	(BRA)		Juan Pablo Montoya	(COL)
24	Niki Lauda	(AUT)		Clay Regazzoni	(SUI)	11	Fernando Alonso	(SPA)
23	Juan Manuel Fangio	(ARG)		Jackie Stewart	(GBR)		John Surtees	(GBR)
	Nelson Piquet	(BRA)	14	Jacky Ickx	(BEL)			

CONSTRUCTORS

204	Ferrari	27	Renault	12	Matra
134	McLaren	20	Tyrrell	11	Prost
129	Williams	15	BRM	9	Mercedes
71	Lotus		Maserati	7	March
40	Brabham	14	Alfa Romeo	6	Vanwall
35	Benetton	13	Cooper		

RIGHT: Mika Hakkinen celebrates winning not just the 1998 Japanese GP, but also clinching his first title.

MOST POINTS (THIS FIGURE IS GROSS TALLY, I.E. INCLUDING SCORES THAT WERE LATER DROPPED)

DRIVERS

1369	Michael Schumacher	(GER)	420.5	Niki Lauda	(AUT)	281	Emerson Fittipaldi	(BRA)
798.5	Alain Prost	(FRA)	420	Mika Hakkinen	(FIN)		Riccardo Patrese	(ITA)
614	Ayrton Senna	(BRA)	385	Gerhard Berger	(AUT)	277.5	Juan Manuel Fangio	(ARG)
527	David Coulthard	(GBR)	360	Damon Hill	(GBR)	274	Jim Clark	(GBR)
519	Rubens Barrichello	(BRA)		Jackie Stewart	(GBR)	267	Giancarlo Fisichella	(ITA)
485.5	Nelson Piquet	(BRA)	329	Ralf Schumacher	(GER)	261	Jack Brabham	(AUS)
482	Nigel Mansell	(GBR)	310	Carlos Reutemann	(ARG)	255	Jody Scheckter	(RSA)
480	Fernando Alonso	(SPA)	307	Juan Pablo Montoya	(COL)	248	Denny Hulme	(NZL)
456	Kimi Raikkonen	(FIN)	289	Graham Hill	(GBR)	242	Jean Alesi	(FRA)

CONSTRUCTORS

3849.5	Ferrari	424	Prost	162	Red Bull (nee Stewart then Jaguar Racing)
3150.5	McLaren	333	BMW Sauber		
2545.5	Williams		Cooper	155	Matra
1352	Lotus	312	Honda Racing (nee BAR)	79	Wolf
976	Renault	288	Spyker (nee Jordan then Midland)	67.5	Shadow
877.5	Benetton			57	Vanwall
854	Brabham	171.5	March	54	Surtees
617	Tyrrell	167	Arrows		
439	BRM	163	Toyota		

MOST DRIVERS' TITLES

7	Michael Schumacher	(GER)	Jim Clark	(GBR)	James Hunt	(GBR)
5	Juan Manuel Fangio	(ARG)	Emerson Fittipaldi	(BRA)	Alan Jones	(AUS)
4	Alain Prost	(FRA)	Mika Hakkinen	(FIN)	Nigel Mansell	(GBR)
3	Jack Brabham	(AUS)	Graham Hill	(GBR)	Kimi Raikkonen	(FIN)
	Niki Lauda	(AUT)	Mario Andretti	(USA)	Jochen Rindt	(AUT)
	Nelson Piquet	(BRA)	Giuseppe Farina	(ITA)	Keke Rosberg	(FIN)
	Ayrton Senna	(BRA)	Mike Hawthorn	(GBR)	Jody Scheckter	(ZA)
	Jackie Stewart	(GBR)	Damon Hill	(GBR)	John Surtees	(GBR)
2	Fernando Alonso	(SPA)	Phil Hill	(USA)	Jacques Villeneuve	(CDN)
	Alberto Ascari	(ITA)	Denis Hulme	(NZL)		

MOST CONSTRUCTORS' TITLES

15	Ferrari		Renault
9	Williams	1	Benetton
8	McLaren		BRM
7	Lotus		Matra
2	Brabham		Tyrrell
	Cooper		Vanwall

BELOW: Juan Manuel Fangio collected five world titles in the 1950s. This is his Mercedes at Spa-Francorchamps in 1955.

2008 FILL-IN CHART

DRIVER	TEAM	Round 1 – 16 March AUSTRALIAN GP	Round 2 – 23 March MALAYSIAN GP	Round 3 – 6 April BAHRAIN GP	Round 4 – 27 April SPANISH GP	Round 5 – 11 May TURKISH GP	Round 6 – 25 May MONACO GP
1. KIMI RAIKKONEN	FERRARI						
2. FELIPE MASSA	FERRARI						
3. NICK HEIDFELD	BMW SAUBER						
4. ROBERT KUBICA	BMW SAUBER						
5. FERNANDO ALONSO	RENAULT						
6. NELSON PIQUET JR	RENAULT						
7. NICO ROSBERG	WILLIAMS						
8. KAZUKI NAKAJIMA	WILLIAMS						
9. DAVID COULTHARD	RED BULL						
10. MARK WEBBER	RED BULL						
11. JARNO TRULLI	TOYOTA						
12. TIMO GLOCK	TOYOTA						
14. SEBASTIEN BOURDAIS	TORO ROSSO						
15. SEBASTIAN VETTEL	TORO ROSSO						
16. JENSON BUTTON	HONDA						
17. RUBENS BARRICHELLO	HONDA						
18. TAKUMA SATO	SUPER AGURI						
19. ANTHONY DAVIDSON*	SUPER AGURI						
20. ADRIAN SUTIL	FORCE INDIA F1						
21. GIANCARLO FISICHELLA*	FORCE INDIA F1						
22. LEWIS HAMILTON	McLAREN						
23. HEIKKI KOVALAINEN	McLAREN						

* TO BE CONFIRMED AT THE TIME OF GOING TO PRESS

Round 7 – 8 June CANADIAN GP	Round 8 – 22 June FRENCH GP	Round 9 – 6 July BRITISH GP	Round 10 – 20 July GERMAN GP	Round 11 – 3 August HUNGARIAN GP	Round 12 – 24 August EUROPEAN GP	Round 13 – 7 September BELGIAN GP	Round 14 – 14 September ITALIAN GP	Round 15 – 28 September SINGAPORE GP	Round 16 – 12 October JAPANESE GP	Round 17 – 19 October CHINESE GP	Round 18 – 2 November BRAZILIAN GP	POINTS TOTAL

PICTURE CREDITS

The confetti fell on Ferrari at the last race in 2007, but no-one can predict who'll wear it this year.

The publishers would like to thank the following sources for their kind permission to reproduce the pictures in this book.

Getty Images: /Michael Cooper: 54t; /Bertrand Guay/AFP: 54b; /Mark Thompson: 46; **Google Earth:** 60-77; **LAT Photographic:** 11, 15, 19, 23, 35, 51, 118, 119, 121t, 121b, 122, 123, 124, 125; /Lorenzo Bellanca: 13, 21, 28, 34, 38, 40, 41, 45, 55b, 82, 97, 105, 108, 114-115; /Jeff Bloxham: 37; /Charles Coates: 8-9, 12, 29, 32, 39, 44, 47, 49, 85, 93, 94, 95, 96, 101, 112; /Glenn Dunbar: 14, 16, 18, 24, 26, 50, 55t, 78-79, 84, 88, 91, 92, 104, 107, 113; /Steve Etherington: 2-3, 27, 31, 58-59, 80, 81, 90, 103, 109; /Andrew Ferraro: 6-7, 30, 36, 48, 52, 53, 56-57, 83, 86, 87, 89, 98, 100, 102, 106, 110, 111; /Peter Spinney: 120; /Alastair Staley: 25, 33, 42; /Steven Tee: 4, 10, 17, 20, 22, 55c, 128; **PA Photos:** /David Davies: 99 **Sutton Motorsport:** 43; Illustrations courtesy of **Graphic News**.

Every effort has been made to acknowledge correctly and contact the source and/or copyright holder of each picture and Carlton Books Limited apologises for any unintentional errors or omissions which will be corrected in future editions of the book.